ISLAND CHAPTERS

ISLAND CHAPTERS

Prose and Poetry
ANNA ADAMS

Paintings
NORMAN ADAMS RA

Littlewood
1991

Published by Littlewood Arc, The Nanholme Centre,
Todmorden, Lancashire OL14 6DA
Designed by Tony Ward, Arc & Throstle Press, Todmorden
Typeset by Lasertext Ltd., Stretford, Manchester
Printed by Smith Settle, Otley, West Yorkshire

ISBN: 0 946407 66 5 pbk.
       0 946407 67 3 hbk.

Acknowledgements are due to to *Outposts*, *The Sunday
Telegraph Magazine*, *Orbis*, *Encounter*, *Poetry Review*, the *Arts
Council New Poems 9* anthology, *Pennine Platform*, *Five Leaves
Left* and *Wheels*, where some of these poems first appeared.
One was broadcast on BBC Radio 3's Poetry Now pro-
gramme, and one on a BBC TV Closedown programme.
Some have been set as a song cycle by James Butt. Some of
the prose has appeared in *The Scotsman* and *The Scottish Field*.

The publishers acknowledge financial assistance from York-
shire Arts Association.

Cover: *Study (late afternoon) Rodel Loch*

For Jacob and Benjamin

CONTENTS

—out in the sea about Usenesse in Harrey, lyes an ile callit the Scarpe, fertil and fruitful, guid for corne, store, and fishing pertenning to M'Cloyd of Harrey.

Sir Donald Monro. 1549

—the island of Scarp is a high land covered with heath and grass—

Martin Martin. 1703.
(A Description of the Western Isles)

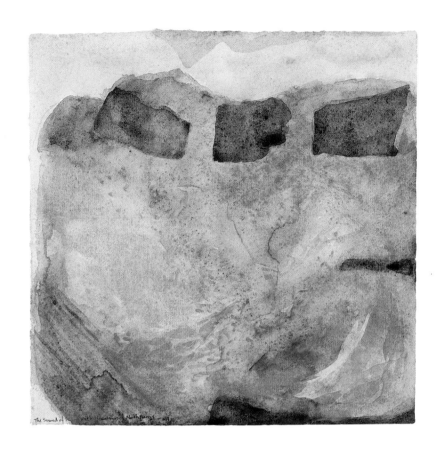

The Sound of Scarp with Mountains of North Harris

1963 . . .

From Husinish, on Harris, where everyone speaks the Gaelic except the sea, which says 'Husinish, Husinish' all day long, we took a weathered wooden motorboat across the green hills of the sea to Scarp.

'Husinish', so an old woman told me in sparse English, is an old Norse word meaning 'the House on the Ness'; and a ness is a naze, or nose, or point of land jutting into the sea. The ness at Husinish is a steep, rocky hill surrounded on all its sides except the East by the unadulterated Atlantic. The Vikings who named it may have found a house on it, but there is not one there now. The houses of Husinish cluster at the foot of the hill, at the landward side. But we left this outpost of the Harris mainland and took to the sea, where the waves heaved with energy as though they were alive, and the children sat tight in their seats, tense with delight as we rode the bucking rocking-horse waves.

On the jetty at Scarp we thanked and paid our boatmen for the ride, and then climbed up the steep hillside of the island. It was as though we had disembarked on the flowery shores of Heaven. Looking back, the sea was madonna blue, the haze-hidden mainland mountains were bald and stony and old, and at their feet a strip of sand shone white. We trod on carpets of flowers – field gentians, bog asphodel, milkwort, speckled orchids, tiny saxifrages, and stonecrop. Ubiquitous ragwort and knapweed vied with one another for pride of place among vivid weeds. Waving crests of green oats, growing in ridges wherever the crofters had been able to build up a reasonable depth of soil, whispered here and there; and laps, ledges and pockets full of summer grass grew among the crags of the hillside. Some of it had been cut and raked into little cocks on the shorn turf.

"What a lovely island," we said to a man who was scything the grass.

"Aye, I liked it well enough when I was young, but I begin to get tired of it now," he said. "The work is very hard, for we have no tractor, and all our fields must be dug by spade. And our young people will not stay. There is nothing for them to do, except to work for no reward."

"Have you no horse either?" I asked.

"If you would keep a horse you must put away two cows, for a horse will eat twice as much as a cow. And then we would not have enough milk. And we can't afford a tractor." He paused. "A tractor would be of no use up there on the lazybeds anyway," he said, pointing at the haphazard hedges of tall oats.

"Why do you call them lazybeds?" I asked, "what's lazy about them?"

"Nothing at all," he replied, "nothing at all."

★

Later we walked along the flower-bordered main thoroughfare of the scattered village, to the post-office. This road was a trodden earth track between vegetable gardens which were fenced with driftwood posts hung with old fishnets.

The Postmaster scrabbled into a jar and gave the children sweets.

"Why don't you stay?" he asked. "There are empty houses here, .the rates are almost nothing, and we have a fully qualified teacher in the school, so the children would get a good education. They would have plenty of individual attention, for there are only four children there now."

His wife also came out to speak with the strangers.

"Shall we keep the children?" they suggested jokingly, but it was a serious joke, for there were no young children on Scarp, and only four in the school. "– And the young people will not stay."

We walked by winding paths down to the shore, where we ate a packet of Post Office biscuits which we gave the high-sounding title of Tea.

I was struck by the beauty of the seaworn boulders we sat on. Some were speckled like eggs, some streaked pink and grey, like sunsets, some tabby as cats, some veined like green cheese, some stripey as bullseyes, and others plain black and glistening with quartz crystals.

"Call them sculpture, take them to Bond Street, and make a fortune," I thought; "readymade art, God is the Best Designer, transport the only problem." I was carried away by my fantasy. I saw the island thriving on the export of boulders, until realising, sensibly, that these beautiful stones were like the treasures gathered in dreams, worthless out of their context.

"Beauty is not art," I thought, "the expression of consciousness is art."

I remembered the higgledy piggledy stones of the strange lonely church at Rodel, in South Harris, the aspiration to immortality of the higgledy piggledy dead that slept under the grass counterpane of the churchyard. Each stone in its fabric was less beautiful than any of these boulders, but they were fitted together by the hands of men into that

10

very human symbol of the cross. Many children's first attempts to portray people resemble crosses. The prehistoric standing stones of Callanish are cruciform in plan. The cross is the symbol of consciousness, which suffers, and rejoices. The egg is the symbol of sleep. These sea-washed rock eggs were as unconscious as they come.

The sun descended behind the island, the wind blew harder and the dark tide rose. The village was on the east of the island; its steep hill cast a long shadow in the late afternoon. Though the sun still shone on the mainland mountains opposite, it was no longer shining on us. I began to feel chilly, and it was borne in upon me that whoever made the world, it was not made for people to feel cosy in, and a stony beach in the eventide can be a very desolate place. Wild landscape can seem anti-human; our environment is people; we live in one another. It is this that makes the idea of Heaven of the young people of Scarp resemble Inverness, Glasgow or even Edinburgh.

"I must leave. How can we stay in this place?" said one, handing us envelopes containing applications for jobs to post for him on the mainland.

And even to me the flowery hillsides of Scarp became dreary when I thought of the island as it might become – uninhabited. For "without Man, Nature is barren."

Interim

That was in 1963, and some fifteen years have passed.

Scarp is changed, and so are we. The boys are grown, and I am living, once again, in that world of work that has no children in it. While children are small and demanding it is often surprising to discover that such a world still exists, and difficult to believe that one will ever inhabit it again. But now I do (with mixed feelings, because women never realise when they are well off) and I am taking advantage of this quiet life to gather together all my Scarp notes and Scarp poems, mostly written since 1969, when we at last crossed the water to the island again.

In the interim we were not without news of Scarp.

Students of my husband's went there, on his recommendation, and some revisited several times, even going at midwinter. They lodged with the islanders, or stayed in a shortlived hostel established in an empty blackhouse on the island. This was not a Youth Hostel, but one belonging to the Gatliffe Trust. This exists to encourage visitors to the lonelier parts of the British Isles. The Scarp hostel is now fallen down, as blackhouses do if not continuously occupied, and its walls are now tenements for mice, starlings, blackbirds, nettles, thistles and goosegrass. While they lived there the students were warmly welcomed by the islanders: they went calling on them in the evenings, and were in and out of island houses 'Just like ourselves', as islanders used to say, later. Two girls in particular, who persisted in going, were very much approved of for their strength and hardworking qualities. Their beauty was less admired, though it must have been noticed. They certainly flirted, and went fishing with the young men on summer evenings; they helped with the sheep at 'fanks', the periodic day-long picnics for the purpose of sheepshearing, or sheep dipping and dosing, or other routines of sheep care in which the entire community participated. One was even earnestly and embarrassingly courted by a young man with honourable intentions who called on her on several Saturday evenings, wearing his best dark suit. He sat awkwardly on a hard, hostel chair, and took tea and struggled to make conversation in English. But English is not the language in which Hebrideans can pour out their hearts, be witty, or pray. The utterly strange, soft, musical Gaelic is their tongue, and in it an English ear can recognise nothing familiar – neither Latin nor Saxon syllables, only the occasional necessary grafting, such as 'social security', 'job creation scheme', or 'Seagull outboard engine'. Needless to say, the sincere young man's courtship in broken and blurred English led to nothing, for ambitious girls have plans of their own, which often come to nothing also, of course. But it was mainly through these two ambassadresses that we heard regular news of the dwindling Scarp community.

Family by family, the people left. The school was finally closed, as children had become extinct. The kindly postmaster, we heard, was awarded the MBE for his services 'beyond the call of duty.' He had crossed the heaving sound whenever possible, to fetch the mails that meant so much to these people right out on the world's edge, whose families were scattered worldwide, though I suppose Inverness and Glasgow must have been the commonest postmarks on the incoming packages. Then we heard that the postmaster was ill: he was wasting away and appearing to be much older than he really was. The illness was leukaemia, so he was compelled to shut up shop and move to a new, breezeblock bungalow on the mainland. And there he died, while the number of households on Scarp dropped from eleven to eight, and from eight to five.

When we at last set foot on Scarp again we stayed for a week in the Gatliffe Trust hostel. We had already spent several weeks camping in our Landrover about Harris: visiting Luskentyre, Rodel, and the bays of the East coast. There the soil is so poor and rocky that the people who settled there after expulsion from the fertile machair of the West, had to build up beds of seaweed to make sufficient good ground for cultivation. The rock is so close under the turf that they have to carry their dead across the island to find soil deep enough for burial.

We had then taken the switchback, single-track, spectacular road from Tarbert to Husinish once again, and we had gone down to the jetty to await the chance coming of a boat to take us over. As we drew nearer to the island we heard rumours that flocks of human exotica were running about on the island. Not just art students, but hippies, millionairelings, old Etonians, we were told, but we didn't believe it. We held on to the image of Scarp that we had retained for six years. What would human butterflies and grasshoppers be doing among the human wild-bees and ants that we remembered? However reduced the population might be, we couldn't believe that the places of absentees were being filled by beautiful drifters in preRaphaelite outfits. But the rumour was not entirely unfounded.

When we had established ourselves in the blackhouse, with campbeds, blankets and Elsanol, as well as free milk from the warden's cow (all for half-a-crown a night), we discovered that the old Post Office, and another of the larger houses, had been bought by rich

13

young men, and in them the young men were entertaining their friends. The houses hadn't been bought for holidays, but to contain an ideal life far from the horrors of civilisation. (Far from the Big Business or the factory farming that assured them an income.) These people were likeable enough, even fascinating, but it is always irritating to meet people who affect to despise work, and materialism, when they are only enabled to dream and play by the unseen labour of others. They needed to toil for apparent self-sufficiency only for so long as hardship continued to be a pleasure to them. So they didn't last. And the ultimate effect of the richest one was destructive, for when he left he abandoned his house without bothering to sell it for the few hundred pounds that would have meant nothing to him, so the weather and the rising damp, and an invasion of nesting mink, are ruining it while someone else could be living there. But this is to anticipate.

I remember saying, later, to one of the young men, that people like us – i.e. artists, or refugees with other distinguishing features, such as money, were like vultures descending on a dying community. Certainly, when the artists move in on a way of life, that way of life is picturesquely anachronistic, and in decay. When artists set up their easels about weedgrown petrol stations, the motor-car will be a vanishing species.

The young man – younger than he seemed, for money is so ageing – replied that he didn't think that they were in at the end of the community, but perhaps might be showing it an alternative way of life. ("With an income, not just Social Security," I thought.) Yet he would not have wished the islanders to become like himself. I think the stability and unselfconscious old-fashioned virtues of the Scarpese attracted these deprived children of the rich very strongly. They adopted the crofters as surrogate parents, as I think we all did, semiconsciously.

I have begun to notice, of myself, that the adoption of parents has been a lifelong habit, and I intend to give it up. Along with falling in love. But that's another story.

★

We spent a week in the blackhouse. There I moved easily and happily into a traditional female role: the primitive house seemed to call this out of me. Then, at the end of our week, Margaret McInnes, who was the official warden of the hostel, showed us over an empty, corrugated zinc house that stood close to her own. We were surprised by the pleasant, airy lightness of this house, for it looked little more than a shed from the outside. The walls and ceilings were lined with tongued-and-grooved planking which made the rooms very warm and well insulated, and the three main rooms rose quite far up into the roof, flattening out into ceiling only about four feet under the ridge, so that their shape was interesting and the feeling of the rooms spacious. As well as three rooms of roughly equal size, there was a lean-to kitchen opening out of the central room, at the back. There was a tap over the sink in this kitchen, but no water ran out when we turned it on. Margaret explained that the pipe had probably been disconnected to fill the sheep dip at the last fank. We took her word for it that the tap was not mere ornament, and many a gallon of wild mountain water has run through it since, proving her right as well as washing our fish or our linen. But we had to replace the pipe. The water supply was provided by a burn running out of the moss and down a rocky crevice in the steep hill at the back of the house. A primitive dam and concrete tank had been constructed to hold back a tiny individual reservoir for the house. The previous owner had been what the islanders called a "knacky" man, able to turn his hand to anything. Lack of specialisation, general handiness, are crofting virtues.

"It is dry," said Margaret McInnes of the house, "it is very dry." And she dismissed the shabbiness of the three-years-empty dwelling: "Bright paint," she said, waving a magic arm, "it needs bright paint."

When I described this vigorous woman of about sixty as the official warden of the hostel, I did not mean to suggest that there was anything of the official about her. She had a strong, rough but very warm voice. She smiled easily. And when we had visited the island in 1963, and sat on the hillside high up above her house, it was a house full of laughter. A lot of this laughter must have been hers. Her youngest child was still only ten or eleven, her sons in their teens or early twenties, and their happy voices flowed out of windows, doors and chimneys on that far distant summer day. Though she was now approaching the boundaries of old age, and had reared five children, she still had the traces of a Spanish-looking, aquiline-nosed type of beauty, and there was still something of the girl about her. Her dark hair lacked a single grey thread, and her weather-beaten face was freshly and ruddily coloured. Her walk was springy as she bounded up the steep hillsides after her cows, and even as she carried the pails of milk back to the house. Though she lacked several teeth and her throat was disfigured by a goitre, her life of hard work (with no indoor water-supply, and only a peat-burning Rayburn, a slender,

15

whitewood butter-churn, and a dark oak spinning-wheel by way of modern conveniences) did not seem to have aged her as much as many suburban women's comfortable (but isolated) lives wither and distort them. She was trusting, kind, hospitable, generous and very active and busy. But she didn't fail to discriminate between people, even in spite of the language barrier. I felt very honoured that she liked us. Her favourite compliment for an outsider was 'homely'. "She is so homely," she would say, "and just like one of ourselves." This is not normally expected of an Englishperson.

★

As a result of Margaret having shown us the inside of the tin house that stood beside her own stone cottage, we called on its owners in Tarbert. We climbed a stony hillside, on the outskirts of the little harbour town, to a pleasant but damp cottage, and after our knock the door was opened by the very man whom we had met on Scarp six years earlier. The man who had been scything his grass had now grown older, had suffered a heart-attack, and was paler from living much indoors. We explained what we had come about, and who had sent us. Asked inside, we sat down in the McLennan's livingroom and Joann made us tea while Angus sucked at his pipe.

"Do you think two hundred pounds would be a fair price?" he asked, after some thought. "Yes," we said, and the deal was done. We had decided, as we drove along the road, that three hundred was our absolute, outside, top limit. So Norman wrote out a cheque there and then, and Angus gave him a receipt, signed over a stamp, which we eventually lodged at the bank.

So the next year we went up at Easter, with brushes and paint, timber, sheets and blankets, a second-hand mattress from the Sally-Army warehouse in Manchester, pots and pans and a new broom. We went again at Whitsun, and for the Summer with our own boat. For we realised that the last of the islanders were preparing to leave, and we knew we must become viable and independent (though part-time) islanders ourselves.

A Map of the Outer Hebrides

I.

A lacy ghost, a trace of drowning land,
of islands holed by lochans
and lochs punctured by islets
all on the point of sinking,
puddled through with water.
The whole, also, ragged
with rivers, bleeds to life.

Perhaps no more than floating foam
dwindles on the bitter sea
that swallows, gem by gem,
its drifting snow, thawed into colder blue.
The islands are a curved sea-scar,
the debris of a smashed wave
wrecked off Europe's rocky coast.
They may be dislocated bones
of Leviathan stranded in shallows,
shifted by tides.
A re-articulated Hebrides
could swim — a supple tadpole —
in the Atlantic pond.

It looks like an afterthought, added to Europe
after the landmass was finished.
"When He had made all the rest
and saw that it was good,
still having some matter in hand
God made the outer islands."
But it was not like that at all.
These afterthoughts were first-thoughts: ortho-gneiss
and foliated granite, igneous rocks
thrust out, molten, from matrix of fire,
and cooled, then crushed and buckled by time,
became these corrugated mountains.

Pressed into the sea
by layer on layer of upstart Europe,
they still keep their heads above water,
are not yet drowned.

2.

A map is not the perfect
platonic idea of a place
like an architect's grand vision
afterwards worked out in mud.
It is an imperfect record
of measurements – length, direction
and altitude, without grandeur:
a diagram of dimensions,
as calendar to year.
A date is not a day
nor a name a man
nor a word the seed of a rose,
so a map is not an island
but only a ludicrous, shrunken
ash of the idea
of lands we saw in dream
rising at the rim
of the jade green dish of the world
full to the brim with sea.

3.

No map can indicate
the cloud crouched along the horizon,
low down, and constant, not cloud
but distant mountains of Harris.
No map can indicate
by deeply indented coastline
the green arms embracing the ferry,
sheilings watching the water,
peatsmoke smell at the harbour,
boulders wrapped in the hillsides,
heather, mosses and lichen
nor eyes of Mrs. McInnes –
blue as the sound she has looked on
all the days of her life.

4.

She has learned this water, these mountains;
she knows the water's mood,
its crescent of breakers, can see
the wind's colour, can read

the rainbows piercing cloud.
She has seen the sun striking Brenish,
waterfall threads stitching Lewis,
the ancient Forest of Harris –
bald as bone, and as white –
and the moon above mountains, its light
glitters in treacle-black water.
She has seen seals swimming like newts
in the clear sound, its blue
stained purple with weed.
How can such eyes retain
a different scene
without this imprinted image
double exposing the page
of her heart, of her brain?

     5.
An overall printed with tiny flowers
covers the island woman's turf-brown dress;
the island wears an apron sprigged with stars.

The island woman wears a flowered blouse;
the island uplands wear a heather shawl
dotted with devilsbit and tormentil.

The island woman following her cow
dabbles her hem in raindrenched clover heads;
the island dips its seapink hem in tides.

The island man is carrying a sheep
about his shoulders like a mountain cloud;
the island lads run all about the steep,
gathering their flocks into a crowd.

The sheep flow downhill in a tumbling stream –
men clip them and they fleece the hills for hay,
for Winter comes to shear the flowers away.

The island woman carries memories
of Summer in her apron. When the gale
keens over the dark island, flinging hail,
she answers it with love and lullabies.

6.

"Like yesterday," she says,
"It seems like yesterday –
"the years go by so quick as you grow old.
"It seems like yesterday." She looked towards
remembered seashore houses, ruined now,
roofless and filled with weeds.

"Black houses were the homeliest: so warm.
"You couldn't hear the storm outside
"and time never hung heavy.
"The Winter was not long.
"It was so safe, so quiet;
"the children played by the shore –"
among the otters' footprints and the birdtracks in the sand.

"The island was full of people:
"houses with smoking chimneys:
"once there were sixty children in the school.
"Old registers are full
"of McInnes, and McLennans,
"MacDonalds and McLeods."
As the burial ground is full
and sinking under weeds,
the stones drowning in daisies.

"First the telephone came, then the road;
"but the road took away the people.
"They're scattered all over the world:
"There's nothing left now to come back to.
"When so many have gone, all must follow."
The people leave the islands.

Early Days

The two Easters and Whitsuns we spent on Scarp while the crofter families still remained are mixed together in my memory. The first was very cold, certainly, and there was both hail and snow. The snow melted away quickly in fitful sunshine, but, while it lay, the vistas of silver islands in a dark blue sea were like the landscape of a different and dazzling planet.

The wind blew down from the North, and the Scarp men took shelter from the volleys of hail in the lee of our house, so a muffled sound of Gaelic talk and laughter came through the south wall while I painted the interior. The boys went out to talk with the men, and they would repeat amusing things that had been said, sometimes commenting – "That's not a bad joke for an old man without any teeth, is it?" But the Scarp jester was not so old as he seemed, but disabled as a result of being blown up, while serving on a destroyer, during the war. Another nail in Scarp's coffin.

Nowadays only the sheep take shelter in the lee of our house in bad weather, but whenever I hear them bumping against the tin wall or rubbing their backs against corners, I remember those last Scarp men leaning against the wall, smoking their pipes and conversing. During those first Springtimes the sheep sometimes invaded our house, for lambs that had been bottle-fed were still very tame when grown, and would follow any human being, even into houses, and they had to be chased out. There were also friendly dogs that came in to tidy up our cat's dishes. People, too, simply walked in without asking and sat down to talk. Some would say, as they came in, "This was my auntie's house," or "My cousin used to live here". As occupants of the house we were almost adopted as relatives. Which was gratifying.

Angus used to come in and sit and talk with the boys, and instruct them in fishing lore. I shall never forget his kindness. On one return journey, while we still used to be ferried by the crofters in their big, clinker-built boat, the sea was fairly rough and he sat beside me and the boys in his black oilskins, and put a protective arm round me, as he thought I might be frightened. Perhaps I should have been, but I never felt afraid but only exhilarated by rough seas in those days. And Angus himself, with his quiet voice, and immensely strong rower's shoulders, emanated reassurance. He seemed the ultimate father-figure. But he was last seen, by us, staring across the sundering sea at the island where he had spent his days, and where Margaret lay buried; and he was last heard of, by us, wandering about the lowland hillside

21

where one of his sons worked as a shepherd, worn out and confused in his mind by illness, operations and sorrow, seeking the house he had built on Harris. But that was some few years later.

There was something altogether exhilarating about those first Springs on Scarp. The birds were active and vocal, and on the move northward. Flocks of geese flew over toward Iceland. Ducks took frantic circular mating flights over the sound. The air was full of whistles and signalling of oystercatchers, sandpipers, golden plover. One morning the boys brought in a shag they had found dying on the beach. It seemed in perfect condition, plump and heavy, with blackish-greenish, viridian-shot, glossy plumage, and clear green glass-bead eyes. It was very saddening that this beautiful creature should have died in such a season, with its bridal crest on its head. Possibly some too-reckless love-chase had broken its neck against the rocks. I drew it, and noted the yolk-yellow lining of its mouth, its scaly textured plastic-webbed feet, and that my hands smelt like codliver-oil after touching it.

There was also the Scarp football season still in progress at Easter. In the evenings all the young males (under thirty or so), would assemble in what had been the school playground, a small field with a fairly large sandy bunker in it, by the old school. There they would play a strange kind of rough and lawless football which our boys found to be much more fun than the respectable variety.

At Whitsun the northern sky used to smoulder all night as though an arctic city were on fire. The sun burrowed along under the northern rim of the world, and at four in the morning it could remain submerged no longer, but would burst from the north-east mountains and dazzle us awake.

The sheep were put outside the village fence after lambing, and Annie McInnes and her son, and Angus and his sons, would be planting their potato patches, and the last few ridges of oats to be grown on the island. The flowers sprang up as soon as they realised that the sheep had gone – primrose, celandine, kingcups. Thrift nodded by the shore; sea campion bloomed in cliff ledges: the ferns unrolled. There was a watercress bed in a stream at the south end, lustrously green; and the turf was suddenly starred with daisies. Margaret McInnes chased her cows to and fro. There were newborn calves, hens scratched about, and the last two young girls of Scarp bottlefed the orphan lambs, or laughed together, brushing each other's newly washed hair in the sun.

Scarp may have been in a state of terminal illness, but its life was still worth living.

Hebridean Study

A Fank: Men Counting and Claiming the Sheep in Spring

In a north-easter, by a white-toothed sea,
counting and being counted in a pen,
the humble grey beasts eddy round the knees
of humble perpendicular beasts, men.

Their dogs grin from the walltop; clipped ears bleed
as the new lambs are claimed: necessity
castrates the rams, doses, daubs blue or red
each bulging-eyed, exploited property.

These mutual slaves together in a fold
of tumbled stones, beside the snarling sea,
are wealth in its beginning, whence the world
gets riches, yet it looks like poverty.

Sea Serpent in Paradise

One reason why we did not return sooner to Scarp was the feeling of melancholy that its very name occasioned when the place was discussed. Always, during the six years between 1963 and 1969, we thought of it as one thinks of a beautiful person with a lingering and incurable disease. A unique and generations-old community was dying of terminal depopulation. Even now, as the west winds of Autumn sweep over these Yorkshire Pennines, making trees hiss and roar like the sea, I think of the loneliness of the last few inhabitants, and of the even greater loneliness of the empty island, locked in the embrace of the great waves that smash against its darkening shores.

Each time a family left it was resented by those who stayed, for it made more obvious the inevitability of their own departure.

In 1971, one man's wife declared herself willing to stay on when all were gone, but "I will not be a Robinson Crusoe" said Murdo, her husband. He had no faith in the permanence of the hippies, and he was right.

We are a sociable species, our survival depends on this.

"When so many have gone, all must follow", said Margaret McInnes in the same year, when her sons were already building a new house for her on the mainland.

We had returned to Scarp just in time to see the last of it.

Our procrastination also had a superstitious foreboding behind it. As well as the sorrow we felt at the idea of a doomed community, my mind harboured the feeling that our return to the island would be connected with a drowning. Perhaps this semiconscious feeling was a suppressed twinge of fear as i thought of the almost perpetual swell in the sound, that undulating cakewalk over sinister depths. It is only natural and sensible to be a little afraid of heights, depths, the unsubdued elements and the sea's immense power, and there is always some anticipatory fear when considering any risky enterprise. We should feel more afraid than we usually do whenever we get the car out of the garage, though habit makes us forget the dangers in our daily lives. Also, anticipation, and looking back on an experience, are usually more alarming than the actual moment of action. Action is exhilarating, while brooding on unperformed actions sets the adrenalin flowing to no purpose. Go out and actually walk the tightrope, and the anxiety disappears, unless you yourself do the disappearing – headfirst into the gulf.

25

Whatever the true nature of my forebodings, there was a drowning in the sound that Summer. The islanders were very distressed by it, and one of the hippies who witnessed it from the ridge of the houseroof he was repairing, packed up and left at once, so it was said.

It was on a beautiful hot summer day, at that time of the month when the tide ebbed very low. Some young people from the south of England were camping at Husinish, and they had walked round the coast by the cliff path to the white beach opposite the village. This beach is half-a-mile long, and nearly always deserted. The bathing is not as safe as it might be, as, when the sea is at all rough the waves break against the steep sand, with an undertow. But on this day the sea was calm as glass, translucently blue, and winedark over the weed. (I never understood Homer's 'winedark sea' until I went to the Hebrides.) As the sea ebbed, the great crescent of sand that all but bridges the sound came heaving out of the water to dry its white back in the sun. From the tip of this horn of sand to the shore of Scarp appeared, from the land, to be a mere stonesthrow. Two tiny pinmen detached themselves from the group of ants picnicking on the mainland shore and walked out onto the sand. They paddled along by the frilly edge of the sea and reached the extremity of the sandbank. Then they waded experimentally in.

"Young men, young men," said Angus, who was on his way to a fank on the other side of the island, "I wouldn't go any further if I were you."

He looked down at the tiny figures from the crest of the ridge where he rested with his boxes of food for the sheepshearers. But he did not wait to see the outcome of the bathe, nor could he have done anything to help if he had. None of the islanders could swim, all of their boats were too heavy for one man to get them into the water, and time and distance would have allowed no help to be given, even if it were possible.

Perhaps it was ten minutes later that Margaret McInnes looked out from her door and saw a solitary bather resting on the end of the jetty in the sun. He had swum across the sound at its narrowest part, and later he had disappeared, so she decided that he must have swum back again. And so he had.

When he returned to his friends on the white beach he found that his swimming companion had not turned back, as he had assumed he had, and as he had neither returned to the mainland nor arrived on the island, he must be still in the water. And that meant underneath it. Then he remembered that there had been a shout – a shout he had not heeded. Now he realised what that shout had meant.

So Husinish was run to, phonecalls were made, and policemen arrived and rowed about in the sound. But not a sign of a body could anyone find.

"It must be the sands have got him," said some. "The current took him," said others. The current can be very strong when the sound narrows down at low tide. "It's no good looking," said the islanders and the police at last, for nothing more could be done.

We had all learnt the lesson, once again, that there is no such place as paradise-on-earth: and one young Londoner had learnt it all too well.

The body was found, months later, right up near Cape Wrath, in a trawl.

And it couldn't have been much of a body.

The islanders were quietly distressed about this event. But what could they have done?

Annie McInnes told me of another drowning, and as it dated from the early thirties I reassured myself, concluding that if they could remember a thirty-year-old accident they didn't have too many.

This, also, took place on a lovely summer day, and also on the day of a fank, so that all the men were over on the far side of the island attending to the sheep. This time it was a woman who stood on the hillside looking back toward the sea. To the north she could see the far white perpendicular of a sail. It was an island boat ferrying a load of sheep down from Brenish, on the Lewis coast. She saw a sudden wind darkening the water, ruffling the sea from the West, and she saw the sail go down. The boat was capsized.

There were two men in the boat. One was young and very frightened, drowning almost at once in panic-stricken struggles. The other was an older man, calmer and luckier. He managed to catch hold of the hull of the overturned boat, and he got an oar between his legs and then hung on for dear life as the boat drifted in the current.

He looked back towards the island while he drew further and further away from it. The peaks of Scarp grew smaller and smaller, but his thoughts of the island grew more and more vivid. The flowered turf, the fishnet-fenced gardens, the crouching houses, the warm red cows, the brotherhood of the people there, all his friends. Everything he had known of life from his boyhood until now: the burns and tarns, the granite stones, his mother, his mother's house; and the firm ground under the islanders' feet as they went to and fro over the mountain, or down to the shore and back again. The flowering machair, the rustling grass and the hiss of scythes. The voices of men

27

and sheep, the warmth of fleeces. The clatter of looms in the weaving sheds, the songs of women as they walked the tweed. His head was full of Scarp.

Meanwhile, the woman who saw the far white sail go down had run over the island to the fank. She told the men what she had seen, so they left the sheep and returned with great speed to the village, to launch a boat and set off toward the North. They set off with very little hope, except, perhaps, to retrieve the bodies.

But they found the capsized boat and the man clinging to it. He had been in the water for five hours, kept alive by a head full of visions of the island, and he was brought back to complete his span of days.

Caolas an Scarp (The Sound of Scarp)

Under milkwhite sea mist
Caolas an Scarp, the Sound,
is violet-blue as a vein
in skin, or a spun-silk skein
of sky. This Atlantic wrist
is a pressure point. Here bound –
with oceanic thrust
from the hidden heart of the round
world's circulating seas –
Earth's primal energies.
Arctics, antipodes
meet here between strait shores
in tournaments of waves
and tidal wars.
From Harbour's sheltering arm
boats feel the galvanic surge
of Atlantic pulse, the urge
of giant hearts drumming blood.
Even when seas are calm
and gently lave
with salivating tongue
the granulated sand,
they still roll boulders round
in currents' coil,
while under cool sea veil,
stained seaweed purple hides
the fire beneath the flood
that boils the tides.

The Boat

We did not buy our boat for pleasure, but as a necessity. As boatmen we were forced to jump in at the deep end, for we had to be prepared to ferry ourselves to and from Scarp when the last of the islanders had left. So we bought a thirteen foot, fibreglass boat of a solid and seaworthy design, and, later, a rubber dinghy. Having transported the boat on a trailer to Husinish, we entrusted ourselves to our own boatmanship. At first this was frighteningly amateurish. I had taken the precaution of teaching the boys to row on the duck soupy water of Platt Fields Park in Manchester; but Platt Fields pond and the Sound of Scarp are two rather different matters.

Without much fatherly advice from Angus McInnes and others, we would not have got on very well. He showed my husband how to put out a mooring, and how to read the signs of the sea's moods. He showed the boys how to disguise fish-hooks with chickens' feathers, and to string eight or so of these cunning devices on to one branching nylon thread, thus making a darrow. This, trailed behind a moving boat, looks like a small shoal of tiny fish and brings in the deluded Lythe and Saithe, sometimes four or five at a time. Even wise old fish, over two feet long, have been hauled, silently protesting, on board a boat already overloaded with perishable first-class protein. In August the darrows lure in Mackerel – a staple of the islanders. It was a staple of ours, too, while on Scarp, but the islanders used to salt their excessive catches down for the Winter; we had to eat ours fresh. We often faced a whole fish each, for every meal of the day, and were always glad if we had temporary neighbours on the island, who might not have had an embarrassment of success with their fishing tackle, so they could be persuaded to accept a humiliating fishy bonanza. On many an evening, now that the boys are older, they set out with half a dozen tasteless fish and knock on a new unknown neighbour's door, to be rewarded – often – by tots of whisky: an exchange which is robbery.

Our old neighbours, Angus and John MacDonald, told us the best places to go for fish – along the edges of the weed patches – and how to put out a plaice line. They told us also where not to go, where the sea is "all dirty with rocks".

The boat may have been bought for utilitarian purposes, but it has had a very important non-practical function. It has been something around which the boys and their father could build up an understanding friendship.

I always felt that the boys saw too much of me, their mother, and suspect that, in general, artists do not make very good fathers. This is because they are producing a rival brood of brain-children all their own. This makes them preoccupied, irritable, frequently absent, and sometimes totally deaf and blind to the needs of their flesh-and-blood children. Unlike a worker on a production-line, or someone clipping tickets in the Underground, they are not working in order to provide for their families but because they are hagridden by their own creativity. Very often nobody wants their products – so provision for families is not something that flows in anyhow. An artist's work is not a means to that end. The business of somehow supporting a family as a side-effect of work, and the nightmare of keeping up with self-employed National Insurance contributions, the necessity to save up to pay an unknown quantity of Income Tax, the formfilling in order to keep bureaucrats in work, and other activities corrosive of concentration, all piled on top of ten-hour days of obsessively seeking for the right colours for the right forms to express the ideas that grow out of each other, leave very little time for helping with homework, taking an interest in meccano, or attending parent-teacher meetings at school.

So it was always I who did all those things, and Norman was a rather remote figure, even though he worked at home.

But the boat made the ideal meeting-place for boys of twelve and fourteen and their father. They could meet there on fairly equal terms. Norman was, of course, the captain, but the ship was run on very anarchist lines. Apart from the boys' rowing, which became much better than their father's, all were equally ignorant. Together they found out about fishing, engines, currents, winds and tides. I backed out of this scene quite early, discovering that being a mere passenger most of the time, my main contribution to the crew was anxiety at the prospect of so much incompetence, which was worse than useless. I also found that fishing-trips were cold, wet experiences, as sundown is the time when the fish seem to be most catchable. And there was an island superstition that women in fishing boats brought bad luck. I willingly accepted this belief and slipped into the traditional woman's role. Not entirely from cowardice. I had felt for some time that I should draw back from the foreground of my sons' lives. It was Norman's turn.

So, from high vantage points on the island, I watched the small white boat snoring to and fro under the far cliffs, or away beyond Fladday. I picked mushrooms to go with the fish. I made the evening fire in the house, and I laid the table for the midnight fish and mushroom suppers. I lit the lamps, if necessary, and I went down to the pier with the knives, and helped with the gutting when the fishermen returned. Sometimes the fish were so newly out of the sea that they would flap under the beheading knife. The surprised heads sometimes lay on the pier with their fins still flittering nervously, until gulls swallowed them down gullets as elastic as snakes. Once the boys caught a small conger in a lobster kreel, and its decapitated head continued to snap its jaws on the pier while the headless body writhed on the kitchen draining board. The boys insisted that we eat it.

Sometimes I became quite angry because the fishing party didn't seem to know when enough was enough, and the pantry shelf would be piled up like a fishmonger's slab. How could we possibly consume that lot before it went bad? But it is surprising how much three hungry fishermen and one cat, plus one cross cook, can eat, so no one ever took much notice of my complaints about the fish-mountain. We fried it, sometimes Jacob curried it, and we invented a fish salad of cold boiled fish, flaked and mixed with chopped onion, chopped mint, diced apple, a handful of sultanas, tinned tomatoes and a little lemon juice. This was very good, but not in the lobster class. The boys eventually succeeded in making their own kreels and graduated to lobster fishing. So we lived, for a few weeks in the Summer, like millionaires.

For what more could anyone do with millions but buy islands and live on lobsters? They could patronise the arts, of course. But we roll our own.

Vikings

Gnarled mountain-roots, long fingers of old rock
enlaced with restless fingers of the sea,
engendered the amphibious Viking stock.

Their world was a great basin full of green
unstable plains and blue ranges of storm
contained by lands conjectured more than known,

and cradling islands – Faroes, Hebrides,
Orkneys and Iceland; Britain to south of these
and, eastward, pockets filled with landlocked seas.

Their skating keels incised in the blue skin
of ocean's roof, the drifting, wavehealed scars
that were their maps, proving that they had been

westward as far as Vineland, where they found
plains of wild corn, and grapes warm to the hand,
and that for us there is no lucky land:

then Vikings turned their keels to plough the ground.

Gannet War

The gannets bomb the seas
in endless battle
to win fish and the prize
which is survival.

Over the breathing deep
each soars to see
the shoals, then tilts, falls steep,
raises brief spray;

bursts, dry, from his wet grave,
shaking his wing
then mercenary brave
gulps silver herring

so gannets may go on
forever fighting
wars that are never won
but bird-delighting.

Blackhouses

For a little more than a week in 1969, on our second visit to Scarp, we lived in a blackhouse. There we arranged our jamjars of weeds, read in bed by candle-light, ate the unsolicited gifts of fish that helped to eke out our strictly rationed corned beef and potato diet, and raised a plume of smoke from the blackhouse chimney as we made bonfires of driftwood in the rusty iron cage of the grate. It was home for us then, our node of security in the wild world; but now it is a rectangle of thick walls, and it looks as out-of-date as Stonehenge. It fell in the Winter between 1970 and '71.

Perhaps it didn't really fall so much as be pushed, because it was no longer safe. But, for whatever reason, the last inhabited blackhouse of Scarp now lies like most of the others, with its inside exposed to the sky, and its rooms, once so cosy, out of doors.

Blackhouses were the traditional, stone-and-thatch, one-storey dwellings of the Hebrideans. Their walls, built without mortar, are immensely thick, and the water which runs off their thatch drains away down the rubbly middle of these walls, so they need no damp courses. They are low, and offer very little resistance to the great gales that blow off the Atlantic, which might topple taller structures. Some are partly hollowed out of the hillside so that only the front walls are built, the back is merely excavated. Many of them are almost invisible from a distance. They all keep their backs to the prevailing wind and allow as small and as few apertures as possible for the superabundant fresh air to enter by, so windows are small, and interiors dark. This is one reason why they are called 'black'. Another is that they usually have a central fireplace and, originally, no proper chimney but a hole in the roof for the smoke to escape by. So they were liable to become very black indeed. Yet the peatsmoke performed a useful service too, in keeping the roof in condition and preventing it from growing a floral hat of weeds which would harbour damp and decay, and cause it to fall.

Yet there is nothing that takes the blackness out of blackhouses so much as the removal of their roofs. This process also takes the house out of them. They become small fields with disproportionately thick stone walls, and an incongruous iron stove set in one of them. Sticks lying about are just recognisable as crofters' broken chairs. Rusty bedsprings proclaim certain small fields to have been bedrooms. Dented metal teapots, full of earth, and fragments of crockery, proclaim kitchens. It is often difficult to believe these proclamations.

But having lived in one, and known it as a house before it became a field with a stove, I have learned to recognise Scarp's other fallen blackhouses. And there are a great many of them. There is a warren of ruins down by the shore, two houses on the hillside north of the jetty, and single ones and scatterings all along the south-east shore where the good sandy soil is. I have counted thirty, and there are possibly more.

Some have doorways like units of a small Stonehenge, their lintels loaded with mosses. In one there is an overboiling of grass and nettles on the rusty stovetop; in another an iron bedstead is covered by a mattress of fallen thatch. A child's toys disintegrate among stones and potsherds. The broken frame of an old loom is still recognisable among the weeds. Celandines grow in sheltered corners of the floor, thistles arm the walltops. Blackbirds and starlings nest in hollow walls which enfold sheltering sheep in hard weather.

The oldest ruins resemble disused nests of birds. They are little more than roughly rectangular hollows in the ground where sheep graze on their fitted carpets of turf. The casual scoops of lapwings and curlews come to mind, and these larger hollows are, in fact, the disused nests of humankind. Their young have flown to the mainland, or further ends of the earth, while elders have gone to the seashore graveyard where all the lettered stones, like all the houses in Scarp, face the sea. This is not from distrust, I realise, but because the East is the site of the sunrise, that symbol of the Resurrection in which the islanders believed. But most of the gravestones are simply boulders, and the number of these stones speaks of what a thriving and self-sustaining community has been allowed to die. I wonder if a permanent, Gaelic-speaking village can ever, possibly, resurrect itself here.

The crofters used to offer reasons for their migration. "It is the sound," most said, yet crossing it had never been easier than it was in the years since the war, when they all had outboard engines, and there was a road to Tarbert from the jetty across the sound. Once they could only reach Tarbert by rowing and sailing round Husinish Point and up Loch Tarbert, unless they walked. Perhaps it was the fact that children had to go to secondary school in that distant township, seventeen miles away, from the age of twelve. There they stayed in a hostel and became used to living away from home, although, as a rule, they didn't like it much. Perhaps it was just that the larger the bodies of cities become the greater the force of gravity they exert on the people of sparsely populated areas. From a distance, probably, city life looks like a lot more fun than it really is. A blanket and generalising explanation is that, as the twentieth century failed to go to Scarp, then Scarp had to go to the twentieth century; so now all the old Scarpese live in council houses with electricity, television and fitted carpets, or they work as telephonists, or nurses in city hospitals, or manage branches of building societies, or are policemen in Glasgow or London.

As I poked about among the blackhouse ruins one Easter, before the last crofter families had left, there was a sound of soughing wings and a crying overhead. A skein of more than a hundred migrant geese flew over, wingtip to wingtip, in long wavering lines that met in an obtuse angle at the leaders in the centre. They passed over Scarp and the glittering blue sound, winging swiftly towards the northern ocean. Soon their undulating line became no more than an almost imperceptible thread waving in the hazy distance. Had I not known what it was, I might have thought it a wisp of smoke; but it was a population on the move, and soon it had completely vanished. Later in the same day another wave flew over. It was their season. And the season for the migration of the little self-contained communities had also come, and a way of life was vanishing.

"It was hard but happy," said the old people of the old times, "hard but happy." And it did not exist fruitlessly, for the success of a society is not measured by enduring architecture, or any material thing or gross product, but the quality of that ultimate product of all production, which is its people. This inclement northern island used to breed co-operative man, which is a far more likeable article than the city product – competitive man. It is strong, ingenious, cheerful, hard-working (he has to be, and so does she), and also knacky, as they say in the islands of a man of many skills.

So the low blackhouses which have become fields with stoves (that have become nesting boxes) should not be thought to have failed. As tools of manmaking they once fulfilled their function all too well. People first began to leave Scarp because the island was overcrowded. Then the community over-exported its stock so that island life became lonely, and the islanders felt cut off. More and more left until they were all gone; but perhaps they carried with them from their rocky breeding ground, to spread about the whole world, their necessary understanding of the law – co-operate or perish.

And not simply with one-another.

37

Blackhouse Woman

1.

I am, myself, the house that shelters them.
My nerves extend into this skirt of stone,
this shawl of thatch. These windows are my eyes.
I am a hollow room, enfolding men.

The peat fire is my heart. This hearth is warm
always, for them, but through the open door
sometimes shy happiness steals in to me.
The sun lays yellow carpets on the floor.

My children bring home hunger, men bring storm,
and I absorb in quiet the sea-bird's cry,
the breakers' roar, till in the sleeping room
oceans and mountains lie.

They leave no room for me in my own womb;
by them, and by their dreams, my lap is filled;
I spread my skirts to shield them, I am home,
content to be my one forgotten child.

2.

They were my life; what is the use of me
now that my fire is out? I smell of soot
not smoke, wear dock and ragwort in my hat,
importune passing mountains of proud sea.

A broken thistle mutters by the bay
that winds have stolen all the seed she bore.
Mine also. Though roofribs, laid bare, declare
me dead, wormriddled, far gone in decay,

my emptiness craves fullness, as the shore
craves the returning tide. I welcome birds,
cherish the weaving spider, suckle weeds;
lacking my lord let nettles crowd my door.

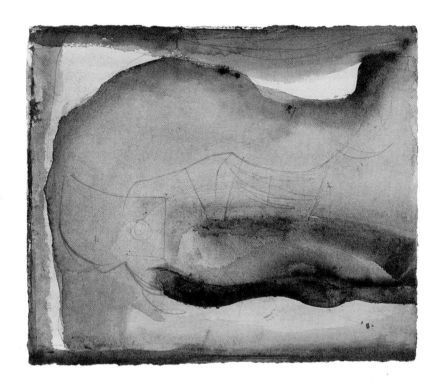

Rocks and Seaweed (Rodel)

In a Roofless House on a Deserted Island

Could she have known as she went to and fro
between the cradle and the fire
between the houseplace and the byre
milking and bringing in dry peat, and so
feeding both babe and fire,

would she have spun this future, to and fro
between the cradle and the fire,
if she had heard the rasp of starling choir
nesting in walls, seen walltop thistle grow,
or grasses pierce her matting with green spear?

Could she have known, for all her toil
and pride, that grass would fill
her kitchen with a field from wall to wall,
and on the stovetop nettles overboil,
and boulders fall

where she, between the cradle and the hearth,
sang as she walked to death,
would she have cared to sweep the weedgrown earth?

The Alternative Society

One hippy household stayed on after the crofters left in 1971, and took the plunge into Winter alone.

They had improved their house, installing a bathroom and a more convenient stove than the ornately scrolled and curliwigged cast-iron Modern Mistress that still stands outside in the weather among grass and nettles, quietly rusting away. The old Post Office already had a water-closet and septic tank, but this house had to be fitted with a lavatory pan and cistern by its new owner. This was done, and all looked very fine inside, but outside the pipe that should have taken the effluent away had nowhere very definite to go, so it humped along under the turf as far as the shore, then poked out of the low cliff and dropped its contents of faeces and pink toilet paper among the rocks of the beach.

This householder had, in his time, taken a trip or two to India, and he had a Guru among his invisible assets: he perfumed the whole island with a mysterious Eastern form of Brylcream, and he owned a boat called the 'God' – presumably because it walked on the water, albeit with a somewhat rolling gait. The name 'God' was written in what he hoped was Gaelic, but luckily it was not quite accurately spelt. This drew the teeth of its blasphemy in pious island eyes. He also had a huge, shaggy dog called 'Siva', which would probably have pleased Indians as little as the 'God's' name pleased the islanders. But the hippy was charmingly oblivious of disapproval: he was far too busy to notice. He invested money and effort in planting trees, and he built solid timber fences round them where there were no drystone walls. He then introduced goats which broke the fences, toppled the walls and ate the trees. He had no intention to be self-sufficient but imported that infallible cure for all ills, brown rice, to feed his family – a devoted and beautiful wife and one small daughter. The child was brought up on libertarian lines, with no prohibitions, which was fine; but the goats were brought up on similar lines, and this was less fine. Goats need discipline, especially indoors.

The millionaireling converted a roofless outhouse into a workshop in which to make arty objects of coloured glass set in metal, which he intended to sell. He fitted a flat roof of corrugated perspex on an insufficiency of beams, and he made a small fireplace which still stands in a corner of roofless walls. For in the first real gale of the Winter after he left, the roof blew away, and for several years afterwards there were fragments of corrugated perspex lying about the island.

41

At the start of Winter he sold his boat, the 'God', but he had another one that he had bought from a departing crofter, and this he used for his last journey across the sound.

"How shall we pull it ashore?" he asked.

"Tie it to the back of the Landrover, and haul it up," he was advised.

So he pulled the heavy, clinker-built boat up the jetty by means of his Landrover. Friends supported it on either side. All would have gone well, but he drove eagerly ahead without looking back, and there is an angle in Husinish jetty. Pulled by the Landrover, the boat's response was to move in a straight line, and cut the corner. So it moved obliquely up the jetty, pushing the young man on the inside of the angle into the water. Luckily he could swim. Then it slipped off the edge and crashed into the water itself, but it had progressed a little further up the pier, so it did not actually fall on the man gasping with cold in the water. It was, however, smashed to pieces on the rocks by the shore, and the hippy family abandoned and forgot it. All the following Summer we were finding pieces of this boat washed up on various beaches. We used them as firewood.

It does not appear that Eton gives its products a very good grounding in knackiness. Leadership? Perhaps, but who, nowadays, wishes to be led? Knackiness? No.

As he was beginning to realise the true rigour of an island winter, unsupported by neighbours, the Last of the Hippies telephoned us at home in Yorkshire, and asked if friends of his could use our house, as he was unable to manage island life alone. (Was it an audience he lacked, perhaps?) He said that the gales blew so hard, sometimes, that it was not simply a question of not being able to go out on the water, he could scarcely go out on land. The wind was sometimes too strong for a man to stand upright. Very foolishly we said 'yes' to this request. It would have been very difficult to do otherwise. So we agreed to lend our tin house to the unknown (though predictable) quantities who stopped by, a few days later, at our cottage in Yorkshire to collect the key for the tin house on Scarp.

After the great departure, when the island Winter had proved too much for everyone, we went up to Scarp in the Summer and found our house lined with a grey layer of sootiness. Obviously all the lamps and the oilstove had been left to smoke, untended. Our stores of wood, coal, paraffin and mantles had all been used up and not replaced. The tilley lamps were all broken, and the oilstove has never been the same again. Items of furniture had disappeared – possibly as firewood – and there was an all-pervading smell of pot. On top of all this we were left not so much as a note of thanks, and the key was never returned. We had to break into our own house and afterwards fit a new lock.

I suppose that to happy hippies, in ecstatic contemplation of the ineffable, materialistic considerations are of no interest; and when the happy hippies have bottomless purses they are quite incapable of understanding that hardwon possessions are of value. For us, most of our possessions are tools of our trade, but trade, even the artist's trade, is not important in Nirvana; nor in the unreal world of Too-much-money. Great discrepancies of wealth devalue the poor man's prized possessions. Big Claus and his four horses can never understand the value, to Little Claus, of his one old nag. The crofter's house could be thrown away by the ex-Etonian when he left, just as though it were a packingcase he had been living in. He never tried to sell it, and, since that departure, only some weekending squatters and the mink have lived in his really charming little two-storey dwelling, with its miniature staircase to dormer-windowed rooms in the roof.

The mink probably found their way in through the open-ended sewage pipe. They have nested, bred and thrived in the house. There are droppinigs all over a torn-up mattress in one bedroom, and their rank odour pervades the whole upstairs, where the hippy infant's toys still lie about as though the family had simply gone out for a walk, on impulse, and stayed away seven years.

Shells

When the MacDonalds left their three-room tin house on Scarp for a council house in Tarbert, it had been a very hard decision to make. The two families remaining felt betrayed: their own departure was now quite inevitable, for the MacDonald family contained two strong young men, newly out of school, who could have kept the island going, had they married and settled down as islanders. It was for their sake that the household left, so that the boys might have a chance of employment.

On the day of departure the MacDonalds went round to each house to say goodbye; there was much handshaking and kissing. At last the women clambered, weeping, into the boat, and they wept all the way over the sound. They wept, and waved, and wept.

It was like a death, for a life was over, and a new identity would have to be made.

So their little tin house, smaller than ours, was left locked and empty, but for abandoned bedsteads, cupboards, a kitchen table, some wooden chairs and a pair of carved wooden lions that a seaman uncle had brought from Japan. Most of the island houses were left like this, with much of their furniture still in them. It would have been absurd to cross and recross the sound with old chests of drawers, home-made chairs and iron beds, and to take a pantechnicon – supposing such a thing could be found – of worn furniture to shame its owners in their brand new home in town. It was simpler to buy new.

This buying of new furniture made an occupation to help heal the wounds of uprooting. "It took us months to get over it," the boys said later. But they did find jobs. One is now a seaman working on coasters, the other works at a garage and lorry-station in mid-Harris. Mr. MacDonald had simply not been able to see a future for his sons on Scarp. But there was no future for him in Tarbert. He remained unemployed, and eventually even sold his boat, then collapsed suddenly one night, and died. He was the man who walked about the hillside on his last days on Scarp, saying – "There's many of my footsteps on this brae," unconsciously uttering a pentametric line.

When we visited the new house in Tarbert we were taken on a guided tour of the new furniture. Mrs. MacDonald switched the electric lights on to show us that they really worked. She demonstrated the flushing of the lavatory. These were strange compensations for the loss of the island and its way of life, though she had not been island-born, and perhaps did not feel it so much.

44

Meanwhile the tin house stands empty, like a whelkshell awaiting its hermit-crab.

But the saddest shell is the stone cottage that stands close by our own house. It was once the last word in modernity, being one of the first white-houses to be built in Harris, a successor to the immemorial blackhouses. Its ground plan consists of two main rooms, one on either side of the front-door which opens into a small entrance hall, running sideways. Fitted between the larger rooms is the small, square, principal bedroom, with a window looking out at the back. Beside this bedroom a steep wooden staircase climbs to the rooms in the roof. There are two of these, lit by trapdoor windows, one on either side of a dark landing used mainly for storage. One of these rooms was the bedroom of the sons, and the other would have been a bedroom for the daughters, but latterly, because the roof leaked, it was used for keeping the tools of a shepherd's trade, for making kreels, and for storage of gear. The second large room, downstairs, was the daughter's bedroom.

Much lighter than a blackhouse, this dwelling was always warm and welcoming when Margaret and Angus McInnes were in charge of it. Margaret had a taste for flowery wallpapers, similar in character to her flowered pinafores. These pinafores were usually covered with very small designs known, I think, as 'granny prints'. They were prevailingly blue in colour, but pale and mauveish with washing. Norman used to find them very similar in colour to the sea outside the open door. The wallpaper patterns were slightly larger, prevailing pink, and femininely pretty. The boys' bedroom, upstairs, was charming with rosy papers when it was still kept alive by habitation.

But dissolution progressed fast once the peatburning stove went out for good. The flowered papers flopped from the walls, revealing tarred paper to hold back the damp in the walls beneath them. Then the tarred paper, too, began to sag and fall. Soot came down the chimney into a mound on the hearth, and a smell of soot and mildew filled the whole house. The ceiling paper lay in one piece over the iron bedstead and marble-topped washstand in Angus and Margaret's bedroom, like a sheet covering the dead.

When the roof falls, and only anonymous walls are left standing, the house will be less sad. And, as things are going, that day is not far off. Meanwhile the house is haunted by benign and homely ghosts, never to be exorcised by new islanders, but only by time.

Five Scarp Sonnets

1. Map of the Paths on Scarp
From every house to every other house,
from every house to Mission-house and school,
a cats' cradle of trodden pathways flows
resistlessly round boulders, and uphill
unwillingly as water, spiralling
from seashore crofts. An Archimedes' screw
of zigzags climbs through crags till, levelling,
it sinks in heather pasture. Down below –
through banks of clover, vetch and silverweed,
funnelled to a plank across a burn
then fanning out, the mesh of footways runs.
But strands are fading. Flow of feet has dried
from roofless walls, weedfilled, that once were wells
of human ways: so now worn machair heals.

2. Tracks
"There's many of my footsteps on this brae –
"There's many footsteps of my fifty years:"
but not as many steps in any year
as many-petticoated orchid flowers.
So many gannets dive into the sea
it should be forested with gannet-tracks
planted on white memorials of spray.
But time's long rain of gannets leaves no mark
but far white crosses diving in the sound.
The weeds of cultivation without crops –
poppies, corn-marigold, heartsease – abound
within the scars of fields. The crofter's steps
are oats and rye grown wild and turned to grass
that springs erect as his few footsteps pass.

3. Knacky Men
Not specialists who fly kites to the stars,
nor mathematic men who plot the course
of rocket-bombs, nor dons and lecturers;
not the fast talkers who arrange our wars,
nor poets, but the quiet knacky men
who can dip sheep, deliver ewe of lamb,

milk cows, make lobster kreels, charm fishes in
with home-made flies, man boats, and make a home
from driftwood planks and corrugated tin,
then pipe in water from a hillside stream:
these will withstand the equinoctial storm.
They can ride out the breakers when they come.
These are the men, the gentle knacky men,
that life would choose should it begin again.

4. Hebridean House
This Hebridean house is like a poem:
crofters' three-chambered shell being sonnet form,
with lean-to kitchen – final couplet rhyme.
Here I inhabit, would make all my own
by painting every surface of it clean
and gathering together in each room
chipped remnants of my mother's crockery,
and faded bedspreads, bought in Battersea,
curtains unfolded from my memory,
salvage of former dwellings. From the shore
we beachcomb saltstained driftwood furnishings:
they enter here like images from dreams
haunting a poem, hinting that they come
with messages from a forgotten home.

5. Symbiosis
Blistering yellow, whitish, crottle grey
of flaking lichen splashes on this stone,
spreading like crusty ringworm cities, are
a symbiosis of algae and fungus, grown
for mutual advantage in this form.
This semi-sunken mountain and the waves
lapping about it, wrapping it in storm,
are a symbiosis too, of mutual loves,
making an island; and the islanders
live in a symbiosis of man and cow,
or man and sheep and cow, like inlanders,
and man and fish, like fisher-farmers. Now
the symbiosis breaks. Divorce is rending
spirit-fibres: life, with marriage, ending.

The Lovely Days

One. A still, warm morning.
Mists like long white French loaves are rolling on the sea. They wrap, unwrap and re-enwrap the low isosceles mountain to the north, and drape the great humps of the Forest of Harris, showing only the gnarled stone toes that they dabble in the sea, and their improbably high crests, leaving all between to the imagination. It would be too far-fetched to say that the mountains resemble squat women wrapped in white towels for modesty, but this might give some idea of the arrangement.

The white garments evaporate or drift away, and in a still land-and-seascape a few crofters and many birds move to and fro about their business. Distant cormorants tread water, rising erect to flap their wings and then fly low over the water. Skuas harry the terns. Oystercatchers, camouflaged in black and white, reveal themselves by flying up with warning cries. Small birds dart about among the tumbled stones where turf ends and beach begins. Flying off, they identify themselves as wheatears by the white chevron above their tails. Starlings, always starlings, make their grating noises about the ruined houses. Blackbirds fly up out of the dark foliage of the potato patch where they have been scratching and probing the sandy ground for grubs.

"When I was a boy," says Angus, whose potatoes they are, "I had to walk right round by the shore to school, for the ground was so covered with gardens."

Not now. Thistles, wild carrots and coarse grass. The dark cities of the burdock. Waste ground. The kneedeep weeds rustle as I walk.

"It's a lovely day, a lovely day," says Mrs. McInnes with real enthusiasm as she takes her milking pails to the byre.

To and fro, to and fro, in the stillness.

The sea at the foot of the cliffs on the opposite side of the sound is dark. There is no line of white foam.

"When there's a black line under the rocks across there," says Angus, "the ocean is quiet."

On such a day as this a small boat might set off for Gaisker, eight miles away. On such a day as this one might even go to St. Kilda. But I – I am not going anywhere.

At evening, while the sun is setting to the north-west, behind Scarp's mountain, the Forest of Harris to the east glows like red-hot coke in the sunset light. The looking-glass sea has the reflections of three pink clouds sunk deep under its green, blue and silver surface layers. The south-east sky is pink in reflection of the north-west sunset, and the sea reflects this reflection.

The snoring of a motor-boat, out fishing under the cliffs, comes over the sound; and as the evening dims into the dusk of a grey Summer night, a large cloud rises to the north-west, frizzy about its edges as Afro-hair.

On such a night, I think, the little boats should hurry home from Gaisker.

Two.

Cloud has overspread the sound, hiding the mountain-tops on either side. Misty rain saturates the machair. Clover heads droop, heavy with water; and somewhere, out in the Atlantic, there has been a storm, for the sea is disturbed.

The silhouette of a heron flaps slow and unperturbed through the mist; it loses itself in the greyness of the sound. Starlings rise from the blackhouse ruins as I go down to the shore. They seem more than usually unmusical, because here they imitate the terns. Our Yorkshire starlings imitate curlews. The terns are fussing raucously over the rocky point opposite the jetty. They are like beautiful fragile girls in snowy dresses who speak exclusively in foul language. Sometimes they are shrilling because harried by a skua, sometimes because alarmed by a human such as myself. But I mean them no harm.

They are grey across the back, they wear black caps, have rose-coloured bills, and, though the rest of their plumage is white, their undersides reflect the green of the sea. They flutter hesitantly, with primary pinions and swallow tails semitransparent and tapering. Delicate in all but language, they dive for fish from a few feet above the water, fluttering in and out like waterproof butterflies.

The sea is grey and uninviting. I have no intention of diving in myself.

Ebbing waves drag the heaped beach boulders back with them towards the deep, the stones clack-clacking against each other in the rush of water. The outgoing wave slides under the approaching slab of water that rears up like a green wall, threatening to topple on me. But I refuse to be bullied into stepping back, and the wave crumbles harmlessly in a heap of exploding foam a few yards away.

There is a game that one person can play with the sea. I invented it. There is really only one rule, and that is very simple. The water should be fairly rough, and the tide rising. The player sits down on the shore line like King Canute, using a boulder for a throne, and

49

must not move until he does so without making any conscious decision about it. He (or she) may rise and run only when to do so is an inevitable and involuntary act.

Perhaps poems should be written in these conditions – only when they are inevitable. Much ink might be saved, and every poem would have the necessary ingredient of desperation in it. It would be something found, not something sought. True poems come into being at the top of an experience chain, as people and birds of prey are at the top of a food chain. But some links of the experience chain may be the writing of manufactured poems, or a poem hunt, and the dark night of the doggerel. Rubbish-writing and despair. It is necessary to work, providing one's own waves of energy, until, suddenly, the poem is given. It may be a line or a word only, but it slots into place like a keystone, locking words together.

But I am still sitting on my boulder facing the sea, and the tall waves are still breaking from both directions, making a rush-hour of commuting waters on the beach. For all the waves that flow forward must also pour back, slipping under the forward and sideways sweeps of surging water. The sea's depth must be built of laminated currents, as is the air's, sometimes. I have seen high clouds moving against the direction of the wind at ground-level, so seeds, fragrances, dust, must cross each other's paths in different layers of atmosphere, just as different people may travel different currents of experience in the same place and at the same time.

I observe that it is not the waves that threaten the most that come furthest. The blusterers break too soon. The tallest green walls topple. The return of spent water baffles many a big one. Cunning accomplishes much. The wave that suddenly, treacherously, pours over the rocks from an unexpected angle, nearly dislodges me. But it is during the sea's quiet, brooding time, when nothing much seems to be happening, that the sea is gathering itself for a powerful and long stride forward . . .

I get up just in time, and from three rapid leaps backward see my throne upholstered in foam.

Returning up the steep hillside that is scarred with old fields and forested with a few dark potato patches, Margaret McInnes crosses my path, driving her cows towards the milking shed. She wears a flowered scarf to keep the rain off her dark hair, and wellingtons for wading in the saturated grass. "It's a lovely day," she says, "so refreshing and cool. A lovely day." She smiles, showing very few teeth, but from behind, as she hurries to catch up with her cows, she looks like a young woman.

On this lovely day it drizzles until the evening, when the wind wakes, blowing from the north where, at dusk, we can see the lintel of the rain spanning the sound from mountaintop to mountaintop. There is also a hole or two in the roof of the blackhouse of the weather; and after dark the sky glows in a continuous northern sunset, until dawn.

Three
Our bedroom faces eastwardly. Very shortly after midnight, it seemed, we are woken by the sunrise. The sun leaps into the sky, dazzling, making a rocket-tail of white fire on the sea. We shut our eyes to defend ourselves from its brilliance, and so sleep again.

★

I go out later, though it is still early morning.

A north-west wind rushes down the corridor between the islands. The sky is swept of all but a few high combings of cloud, and the sun glitters on a sea bluer than ultramarine, greener than viridian, with white hyphens of foam appearing and disappearing in an even pattern all over it.

Mrs. McInnes' washing blows horizontally, flapping rapidly and noisily. It must be firmly pegged, as mine is: but mine now and then jerks loose, and nearly escapes. It hardly seems necessary that anything should be washed – surely the sheets could be hung out dirty, to blow clean in this antiseptic air. But I don't have the courage of this conviction, and have washed, before hanging out, our pink, orange and purple sheets, foreign flags in these parts. The water is so soft that it practically lathers at the sight of soap; rinsing is the difficulty, particularly as the water supply tends to dwindle to a trickle after much use. But hanging out the washing, so it flaps and scatters sparkling showers over a wide area of clover, is a joy.

The waves, with the wind at their backs, hasten down the sound like rush-hour crowds over London Bridge – the one that was dismantled, transported, and re-erected over some dry space of America. The islanders think that the bridge should have been brought here. Two such bridges would span the sound; but could their piers be rooted on these shifting sands? For the sound is all but bridged already, by an arc of sand piled up by the waves coming round the island from both directions. The sea banks the sand up where the

Mist over the sea – Rocks and Headlands – Hebridean Study

currents meet. When the tide is very low the bank is only just below the surface, and it captures, sometimes, unwary boats which have to await release by the returning waters.

This sand-bridge looks very beautiful – a pale crescent under the water where the waves break across the sound – but it is not to be trusted. The water runs fast through its deep green gaps, and though it shows above the water in places, these are different places every full moon, and the sand is often infirm underfoot.

So the islanders desire a proper bridge.

"It's all very well in Summer," they say, "but you should see the breakers in the Winter. No boat can live in such breakers. They reached the boats, on shore, one year, and damaged several. And they took MacLennan's boat and tore it up as thought it was made of paper."

"When it is wild, in Winter, we are prisoners of the sea."

But today is a lovely day – "So fresh," says Mrs. McInnes, returning from the byre with her pails of milk. She leans against the wind and talks about past Winters. I begin to understand the rules of the game. The whole Summer is a lovely day after the Winter's night. But, of course, she hastens to add – "In Winter the weather is often good, we have some lovely days."

For who are we to criticise the changes of the weather? We cannot take exception to some of the notes that add up to the cosmic music. We should not add whines and complaints to the concert, but listen, and keep on listening, and we may hear the tune. Mrs. McInnes, for all that her life might be thought to be hard, appears as though she hears it, and finds it beautiful.

"A lovely day," she says, picking up her pails of milk.

"A lovely day," I say, repeating the lesson that all days are lovely.

Hebridean Sabbath

Painted with rust, or grey as sea,
one-storey, corrugated-tin shacks stay
quiet as limpets at low tide, all day.

The Sabbath closes doors and hushes speech,
manacles hands, gyves feet, suppresses each
workaday wish for play, deserts the beach,

while people from the seashore houses wear
their Sundaybest expressions, oil their hair,
and walk in polished boots to meet for prayer.

Morning till evening, in swept living rooms
of every silent house, they welcome home
the One who made the world, and honour Him.

So, through the week, He, with them in the boats,
pulls in the fish, and grows green crests of oats
in hillside lazybeds. Where far bright floats

Mark lobster kreels, He lures the prizes in;
always aware of Him, he cares for them,
even in cockleshells tossed by the storm.

And, from steep islands, women frequently
see God out walking on the wrinkled sea,
or, on high ledges where they scythe the hay

He runs in eddies, like a child at play,
on flower-carpets where the hailstones lay.

What's Done Cannot Be Undone

The tide crawls forward now
washing the beach more thoroughly
than might seem necessary.
One wave, I think, would be enough;
but, obsessed, the scrubbing arm
sweeps round wide arcs of foam.
Returning water files through crevices
and shakes out weed to lay it slanting seaward.
It polishes, repeatedly, meticulously dries
already spotless sand. You might think it erased
an army's footprints, or deodorised
the bed of a mass orgy.
But almost no one has been here.
A gull or two flew down and stood about;
a chain of three-toed tracks
wavers along the shore.
Last night an otter scurried round the rocks
and ran into the sea.
Perhaps a few small necessary murders –
such as maintain the world – have taken place:
nothing that warrants this
fanatical twice-daily cleanliness
of waves destroying evidence of guilt
but not the spot itself. And waves forget
that they have washed all proof away.
Only their own faint overlapping tracks,
like tiles laid upside-down, remain.
So, tirelessly, the tide begins again.
Last Winter, not remarkable for storms,
it scoured a beach of sand away.
The sea lathers my feet. As I step back,
it sets to work on my few idle marks.

Hebridean Nesting Sites

1.
Here water nests
high, high above sea level,
beside the eagle

where broody clouds
fold grey rain-wings and sit
on tarns to incubate

their crystal seed
which feeds on sky, and grows
until it overflows

steeply to shores
where, perching at low tide
in rockpools lined with weed,

sea-water roosts.

2.
The sea ejects her granite roe
inland, on moss beyond the beach,
and heaves in equinoctial throe.

Her labouring muscles gather, flow
through limbs with a long reach.
The sea ejects her granite roe.

Sun-hatched, these ringstraked sea-eggs grow
yolk-yellow plumage till waves snatch
and heave in equinoctial throe

ragwort and camomile, strip, show
bare boulders. Flower-bones bleach.
The sea ejects her granite roe
and heaves in equinoctial throe.

Another Day

The shaggy dog Siva lollops disconsolately home along the shore. His master has gone off in his boat to fetch peat for the Winter, and has left him behind, so he returns to guard the house. He isn't a proper island dog, his owners are new-islanders. Island dogs are black-and-white collie sheepdogs. That is what an islander means by the word 'dog' – an eager, browneyed, trained companion and servant. And he calls it by such names as 'Judy', or 'Potato'.

By 'cat' islanders mean a grubby white mousecatcher that slinks in and out of houses on sufferance – for all island cats are white.

But Siva is an old English sheepdog, and in some ways, notably his fleece, more like a sheep than a dog. He is large, looselimbed and hidden inside a woolly great-coat. Abominably snowmanish, pig-eyed and unhygienic, with various kinds of manure swinging in his hair, he has a demonstratively affectionate nature and is adored – often hotly defended – by his owners who are hippy-style longhaired crofters whose staple food is brown rice and whose religion is also imported – from India.

Inspired by the dog's name, I looked up the original Indian Siva, who bears no resemblance to his namesake, and I discovered the God who dances.

Siva embodies a beautiful and profound idea. He is ascetic and yet a god of fecundity. He creates and destroys. He is neither kind nor cruel, but beautiful. He is neither good nor evil, and can draw demons into his dance, but in the patterns of the dance the evil is neutralised. He can swallow poison, and assimilate it, so it becomes a part of the dance. He has six arms and a necklace of skulls. He is like Time; he is the law behind the organisation of the great clock of the universe. He juggles with suns. The galaxies are his bracelets. The sea is his scarf, the night is his veil. This Summer is embroidered in a fold of his robe. We glimpse it for an instant as the dancer flies past. He cannot stay. Indifferent to suffering, he dances on, and people may be trodden on, or worn out, in the dance, but the dance continues. There is dissonance in the music, but the music is beautiful. Siva dances.

He has a third eye in the centre of his forehead. It is usually closed, for when he opens it he sets the Earth on fire, but this is no disadvantage to him, for with it he sees phenomena from within.

I do not think Angus McInnes, now hoeing his potato patch near the ruined house by the shore, would allow himself to give a minute's thought to a heathen god; but I think he would understand the idea, if he did, that he is himself a movement in the great dance – and an observer also.

He is always so calm – so accepting. The expression on his face often suggests that he has his own hot-line to God. He appears to be listening, and his serenity suggests that he knows that the totality of experience adds up to a great dance. By living always in one place he sees Summer and Winter changing sides – the sun rising and setting further and further to the North in Summer, and further South in Winter, till there are scarcely three hours of daylight. He sees the full moon rising, vast and pink in the sunset light, over Husinish in August, and setting like a broken coin, snapped clean in half, towards Iceland, some days later. At the Equinox the winds rage and the sea is disturbed, but there is no rough sea that does not go down. Duststorms of birds fly north in Spring and south in Autumn, their movements ruled by the shadows of the beads of the great dancer.

But Angus is very far from heartless. He still mourns those of his friends who, as seamen, failed to return from the second World War. He says nothing, but he heaves a deep, involuntary sigh when the war is mentioned. "No, they didn't all return," he says. Many Harris men went into the Navy during the war.

Angus is the Elder of the Village of Scarp, and immensely dignified and respected here. Yet there has been a time when he went away to work with a road-gang at Fort William, to raise money in hard times. I shall look with new eyes upon gangs of labourers in future, for they may be princes in their own country. Princes and wise men. Angus also leads the service in the Mission now that the island no longer supports its own minister. When we first came over in 1963, there was a missionary crossing the sound in the boat with us. He said that he had dreaded coming to so remote a parish. He had been almost ill with fear of the loneliness; but the islanders were so kind, and made him so much one of themselves, that he had never been happier anywhere. But nowadays it is usually Angus, the village elder, who takes the services. There are two per day on the otherwise totally silent Sabbath. He reads out of a big book of Gaelic sermons, and when he has read through all of them, he returns to the beginning again. But just now there is an English Methodist minister on holiday in the disused Mission House, and he takes the services, and preaches sermons enlivened with references to the events of today – the strangers, artists, fibreglass boats, the strange shaggy breeds of men and dogs. He even spices his sermons with wit. And the depleted congregation sings its strange Gaelic hymns in parts, as they have done all their lives, with shrieks and drones like a set of human bagpipes.

But while I have been writing the shaggy dog Siva has arrived home. He cocks his leg against the corner of his master's house, scratches himself, and settles down to pass a long day's wait in sleep.

For Margaret McInnes

1.

What prescience made me sure
you could not be transplanted?
For me, you were the island,
rooted, as is the island,
in rock beneath the seabed.
Rooted you would endure –
most courteous and kindest,
most welcoming great lady
that ever milked a cow.
So generous, so gay,
your poverty was plenty;
more than enough was riches
enough to give away.
You gave us milk and crab-claws,
eggs when you could spare them,
and time and tea and talk;
you were the Queen of Scarp,
and yet a child on Sunday,
so chastened and so tidy
but loud to sing and pray.

2.

I thought I had been wrong.
You settled in the house
your sons built on the mainland:
electric light and drainage,
breezeblocks and plasterboard,
a bathroom, a new toy.
You showed us how the flush worked,
full of joy.
You planted little trees;
you had begun a garden.
The most essential plantings
were fencing-posts, or sheep
would nibble it to nothing.
"Wild swans came to the tarn
sailing on great white wings
in Spring," you said with pleasure,

"and reared two young, and herons
stand fishing on the shore."
"She would not go back now
for anything," said Angus;
" — and vans come to the door
with groceries, and hardware.
Everything I wish for."

      3.

I thought I had been wrong,
but every night, in dream,
(I know now), you returned
to "Flowerbank" on Scarp:
to hillsides where your feet
knew every boggy patch
where Iris grew, and Kingcups:
every erratic rock
or outcrop crag, or burn.
You did not pine at all
for when you crossed the sound
your essence stayed. New life
was afterlife, you died
when you moved house: appeared
to move and live in exile
but you could not be moved.
I understand it now.
One night, after a year,
you simply stayed on Scarp
continuing your dream.

      4.

Who guessed you would return
so soon to your true home,
and the boat of your return
be your boatborne coffin?
Mourners came from far —
from Tarbert, Oban, Glasgow —
converging on the pier
to cross the heaving water
crowded in boats together
like little public meetings
assembled on the water.

61

They carried up the shore
your shell; you welcomed them,
for you were here before,
awaiting their sad coming.

5.

The eagles of Strone Romul
observed the chapel spilling
a cluster of black digits
that carried a black minus
slowly across the sandhills.
Processional, they followed
the coffin to the gravemound
studded with seashore boulders.
Dark, among the white stones,
the digits stood; they buried
a daughter of the island,
a mother of the island.
She sleeps now with her village –
the past of all her village
compressed into the present,
contracted to the graveyard
honeycombed with coffins
containing men and women
whose feet knew all these hillsides
as hers did, whose feet trod
the ways between the boulders
the steep track to the mill
the winding tracks to school
the broad path to the chapel
the valley to the gravemound.
Now all the past is gathered
the island is translated,
laden with sleeping cargo,
into unchanging seas.

In the Doorway of 'Flowerbank'

Several times, while you lived,
I mistook your doorway for mine.
Now, behind me, your rooms
decompose. Malignant damp
erupts in the floorboards, and mice
erode woodwork with chisel teeth;
they keep disorderly house
in mattresses, cupboards and drawers:
unweaving, unjoining, unspinning,
unpicking, teasing and shredding
the ordered human place.
Your bedroom ceiling-paper
has flopped, whole, over the bed,
and covers the room's dead face.
In a kitchen of rags and rot
flowery papers have peeled
from the plaster. A slagheap of soot
half-buries the rusting grate.

With my back to your dead-house door,
I wait here, where you have watched
for almost forty years,
and, summer after summer,
have seen what I see now:—
that arc of green breakers, and clouds
floating their rafts of shadow
on level seas, or walking
across them on stilts of rain.
Rainbows, and broken rainbows
propping the beam of cloud
over your three grown sons
at work in the sea's far corners —
their boats small as water-beetles
by chalk-scribbled warnings of rock.

While I stand here as you did,
to watch my own sons fishing,
perhaps you will mistake
my eyes for yours, inhabit

my head for a short visit,
so I may know your mind
and guess your well-kept secret
of keeping nothing in your generous heart.
But you have kept no wish
to haunt, or use, my eyes:
your life burned without ash.

Deserted Island

Since people left, corncrakes move in
to nest in deepening grass between locked houses.
I hear at night, each time I wake,
the creaking of the crake
like croaking frogs, or like a telephone
at the distant end of the line.
It calls and calls, again and then again;
yet is not quite that desolate
repeated call, unanswered, in a house
which people have left forever, where people lie dead,
or are, and have been, all their lives,
both deaf and dead to urgent summonings.

The corncrake calls and calls; the double note
signalling other crakes.

I saw one, stepping, cautiously, through grass,
followed by what I thought at first were mice –
dark-mottled little crakes.

This rock may shrug its people off
but it is populous.
Withdrawing itself within a purdah of rain
the island pulls mist-curtains close.
Behind gauze veils we hear the giggling birds
and chattering of burns in dialect
as they run seaward, flowing over grass,
shouting like gutter-children mocking middle-class
intruders in their district.
Out in the rain, stepping across the burns,
I find the ground is mined with snipes.
Touched off, they panic up
to ricochet off nothing as they fly.

I lie awake. The corncrake calls all night.
Its voice, if it is a voice, saws like a file
working through prison bars.

Mist

The boys were all fishing under the cliffs; and close to them our neighbour Brian was anchored and fishing with a rod and line. I glanced over from time to time, for the sun was already low behind Strone Romul, and casting Scarp's shadow across the sound, darkening the lower slopes of the mainland mountains. There was also a certain milkiness in the air over the sea. It wasn't a mist that was blowing in from elsewhere: there was no wind. It was mist condensing in the air. While I watched the atmosphere was turning opaque, just as clear water does when disinfectant is poured in, although both fluids are transparent before they combine. The cool of the evening added to the transparent evaporations of the day caused this unforeseen thickening of the air. I began to grow anxious. The fishermen ought to come over before things grew any worse.

Just then I heard our engine revving up, and the now dim white hyphen that was our boat moved purposefully in the direction of home. I fetched the fish-box, the roe-plate and the gutting knives, and went down to the jetty. By this time the boat was at the mooring, and the long-drawn-out tying of secure knots, and transference of fish into the dinghy, was taking place. But Norman and the boys were only just visible fifty yards from the shore. Their grey and ghostly shapes clambered from one boat to the other, and the creak and splash of oars brought them quickly towards me, so their forms regained substance and three solid people came ashore. We all carried the dinghy up the slipway, and as we did so we could hear Brian's engine approaching. We expected to see him as we gutted the few fish, but we saw nothing but a white wall of mist a few yards from the island: yet we had heard the engine quite clearly, and Norman said that he had shouted to Brian as he left the other side, and he could hardly have been unaware that the air was thickening like custard. He had, in fact, seen him pull up his anchor and start for home. So we didn't worry unduly, but took our fish up to the house and set it to sizzle in the pan.

Just as we were clearing away our fishbones there was a knock at the door. Brian's wife stood outside. Brian and his crew had not come in. Had he said he was coming over? Norman told her that he had seen him set off.

"He was right behind me; or so I thought."

"So he should have been home an hour ago."

We all went down the darkened hillside to the jetty, and we shouted, and we listened for engines. Sometimes we thought we had heard something; then we realised we had heard nothing. The snoring of the sea can sound remarkably like an engine at times.

We fetched a storm lantern, and waved it. We held it aloft as a kind of embryo lighthouse, and it illuminated a little of the mist. It created a small world like a cottonwool snowball with a group of anxious people inside it. We shouted again. If we were answered at all it was by echoes, or humorous seabirds.

It was perfectly futile, but Sheila wished to wait on the pier. She felt happier staring at the mist, and hoping for the shadow of a boat to emerge from it, than she could imagine herself feeling if she sat indoors. Yet she couldn't stay on the pier much longer, for her children were sleeping unattended in the house. I volunteered to go up and babysit, as she couldn't be in two places at once; so I sat by her fireside in relative serenity – for it was not my husband who was missing – and Sheila waited on the pier in a state of mounting anxiety. Later she came in and we both sat by the fire. She fetched the sherry bottle and, by degrees, we emptied it. We discussed all the possibilities (except the ones we didn't dare to name). The sea is calm, we said. There is no wind. (But he could still be drifting out on the current, into the open Atlantic.) We all have a stupendous will to live, we said, and when hard-pressed can be very ingenious and resourceful. Even the most suicidal of us fight for life when up against the elements. He's not a helpless booby. There are islands everywhere about. One is more likely to find dry land than the open sea in these waters. He's probably sleeping out on the beach over there, waiting for the mist to clear.

The moon was in its third quarter and due to rise at about eleven that night. "After moonrise", I said, "things will improve. We'll go out between eleven and twelve and see what we can see."

I must have had an unscientific notion that moonlight might dispel the mist, as sunlight would.

Sheila's children were fast asleep, the sherry bottle was empty, we had discussed all possibilities but the unmentionable one, though it haunted the background of all our publicly paraded ideas; and Sheila must have run through the contingency plans for widowhood that women always have up their sleeves but feel ashamed of. It was eleven-fifteen. Norman had dropped in for twenty minutes and returned home to finish the washing up. Jacob and Ben had long been gone to bed. Sheila had been again to the pier, where we had left the stormlantern as a kind of forlorn hope, and the waning moon must by now be climbing the sky. When we went outside the mist was whiter and more luminous because of the moonlight, but it was no less opaque. It was simply more visible, but it was noticeably thicker down by the water than uphill round our houses, so I decided to climb up one of the nearby knolls and see if it grew clearer still.

Quite rapidly the mist grew wispy and threadbare, and I emerged into bright moonlight. From the top of a rocky hump I could see the mountains of Harris and our own grey, moonlit landmass cut off at the knees by a white sea of fog. It was as though sea-level had risen by about a hundred feet, and the risen sea had turned to porridge. A layer of mist covered the sea like the cream on top of milk, but above it the air was perfectly clear, the sky starry, and the moon, a slightly swollen half, soaring up above the eastern mountains. Somewhere underneath that smothering featherbed of mist were Brian and his friend in their absurd rubber boat, for there were no signs of human life on the reduced black hills that rose from the white flood.

As I descended into the mist again my sharp, mooncast shadow dimmed and died. I returned to Sheila to suggest there was nothing else for it but to go to bed and (if possible) sleep.

I hate to think what sort of night Sheila had (I know that there are times when even death would be welcome as a relief from anxiety), but I slept very well, being dog-tired and full of sherry. We rose at dawn and went straight out into a pale pink sunrise. It was one of the most beautiful mornings I have ever seen. The storm-lantern's orange and smoky flame still burned on the jetty, looking tawdry in this luminous mother-of-pearl world, and the highly polished moon now shone high in the sky. The sea gleamed like satin, calm as a pond. A distant cormorant stood up in the water and clapped its wings. Various sea birds went about their business. But there were no boats and no people to be seen on land or sea. Brian and his friend, and their boat, had evaporated with the mist.

We stared and stared at the empty sound, at the uninhabited hillsides, the far-off islands.

Then we admitted the necessity for breakfast. I suppose that after breakfast we would have gone to Husinish and raised the alarm. Perhaps we would have gone before breakfast. It was still not yet six. But as we prepared to sizzle more fish, Sheila came knocking again. She had seen headlamps flashing by the jetty at Husinish. Taken by surprise, she was not perfectly sure of what she had actually seen. It may have been sunlight reflected in the glass of the cars. It may not have been their own car that flashed its lights. But she had seen something.

Then we spotted tiny figures crawling along by the cliff path from Husinish to the beach opposite. They disappeared among rocks, then reappeared; at last arriving at the beach. From a cluster of rocks the oilskinned ants produced an object, which they dragged down to the water's edge, then launched. An engine started – unmistakable in the stillness – and the boat drew nearer over the flat-calm sea, its wake forming a homeward speeding arrow on the empty water. Soon a very sheepish Brian was slinking ashore.

In proper English fashion we backed out of the emotional scene that ensued, and went home to a really huge and hearty breakfast. Later we heard what had happened.

When Brian pulled up his anchor, only a minute or two after Norman's departure from the fishing-ground, he set off in the wake of our boat. But the air thickened rapidly. By the time he reached the middle of the sound he had quite lost sight of us. Scarp itself had disappeared, and the mainland behind him had also vanished. He kept on going, as he had no alternative, but never seemed to arrive. The crossing was surely exceptionally long, and no land appeared ahead. "Surely we must be over by now" he and his friend kept saying to one another. But the boat droned on and on, till at last a few rocks appeared. They were lapped about by shallow water, and beyond them was a sloping beach where five or six seals reclined like bathing beauties on the shore. Land ho. Perhaps this was Circe's isle, and the seals were really ex-people. But the two men did not land there and then amongst the wallowing seals, but, guessing that they had made a wide half-circle in the mist, and had arrived at the northern end of the long white beach, they puttered cautiously along the edge of the water, as though their curving route over the water were a great bow, and now they were travelling down the bowstring. They passed by more surprised seals who stared at them reproachfully from land and water until they reached the southern end of the beach. Then they landed, pulled the boat ashore, hid it among rocks and set off along the cliff path to Husinish. Halfway along this path they lost their way by climbing up a stream that falls through a steep gully to the sea. But when they had climbed up out of the mist they realised what they were doing, and, getting their bearings once more, they made their way along the track to Husinish. Deciding against spending the night supperless in the car, they went to the nearest house and explained what had befallen them. They were given supper, sympathy and a night's lodging; and the lady of the house refused to take any money for her hospitality, for such adventures may happen to anyone who has dealings with the sea.

Later, others told us of similar adventures.

Once three island brothers out fishing in a small boat were overtaken by a sudden mist that wrapped about them before they knew it was coming, and they were hopelessly lost in the middle of featureless waters. They rowed quietly along, with no sense of direction at all, until they came, by chance, to the shore of a strange island. They landed and pulled the boat ashore, and stumbling up the beach came upon a tumbledown stone wall. They settled themselves in the shelter of this wall for a cold and uncomfortable night's sleep on the ground. When they woke in the morning they rose and stretched themselves to ease their aching joints, and, looking over the wall, saw their own house. They had been unable to recognise their own home in the mist. And they were islanders.

Murdo McInnes suggested that a boat could be kept on a straight course by the dropping of pieces of broken stick in its wake. As one piece drifts away from the stern, drop in another. While you can see three you can tell if your course is straight or not.

No one mentioned anything so sophisticated as a compass.

Rocky bay – Scarp

To Moil Mor Beach

Scarp's wave of land rears out of the sea from the West and breaks towards the East, so that the steep hill behind the settlement of houses is a jagged granite wall, cracking and falling, in very slow motion, into dramatic crags and crevices. The tumbled heaps of broken stone and leaning cliffs suggest an earthquake; but it is all really part of the slow, continuous earthquake in which we live and, somehow, feel secure.

So the path up the near side of this ridge, wave, or small mountain at the back of the village is as steep as a flight of stairs. In Yorkshire the way over would be called a 'nick'. There is a dip in the skyline to be seen from sea-level, and a zigzag, hairpin-bending path ascends towards this valley gouged across the crest of the hill. Between the tilted bedding-planes that form the walls of this nick there are peat-bogs, deceiving moss mats concealing dark brown pools; heathery lawns sprigged with orchids, bog-asphodel and devil'sbit, in their seasons; and in crevices of the steep walls grow dripping liverworts, ferns, and some of the few tenacious Scarp trees. There is a kind of poplar with round leaves that makes a sound like falling water in the least breeze, as if there wasn't enough real water descending from the saturated mosses already. There are also honeysuckle and some desperate briar roses; but both wind and sheep discourage ambition in trees.

Splashing through the shallow pools, crunching over the sharp broken granite, keeping to the fading crofter path which avoids the more sinister bogs, one comes to the end of the cutting through the hill's brow, and then the boulder-strewn moorland slopes and slides down to the shore, so one walks easily over the springy heather and ubiquitous tormentil, no longer pausing for breath but to admire the botany: Butter-wort and Sundew with its redlashed leaves.

Small flocks of golden plover fly up, and a hooded crow flaps past with a scornful cry as I walk down the manscarred areas of the lower slopes. I step over the pink flowers and purple leaves of lousewort in the damp troughs between old lazybeds. There is a shallow tarn, its waters starred with marsh buttercups, overflowing seaward in a valley near the shore. But flowing out of the large tarn that lies, cradled high up in the heart of Scarp, between this lower hill and the great crags of Strone Romul, a fast-flowing burn winds between rocks, divides, pours over falls, joins up again, incises a deep channel through

72

the turf and descends to the Moil Mor beach. The course of this clear-voiced stream, always full and in a hurry, is not quite so haphazard a result of its own whims as at first appears. Here are traces of man at work. This wild water has been dammed, diverted, and harnessed to a millwheel – now vanished – to turn these great millstones that lie in a round and manmade chamber where the stream eddies about and then refuses to stay. Here was the mill that gave the beach of Moil Mor its name. But it has not been used in recent times. None of the living crofters remember it. There are also traces of a roadway, fit for pack-horses or mules, round the southern shore of the island to Moil Mor. And down by the rocky beach, where the millstream flows between small level fields and disappears under the gigantic potato-boulders of the beach, there are signs of man in plenty. Lazybeds have been cultivated here within living memory.

In 1971, my elder son being fifteen, and desiring a greater independence and more privacy, brought his small tent to the level ground close to Moil Mor beach, and slept here alone every night, climbing back over the hill each morning for breakfast. Several of the crofter young men said they would never do such a thing. I don't know why. Possibly they were afraid of ancestral spirits from the old times, or kidnappers, or sea monsters, or sudden and dreadful tidal waves that might come surging up from the sea in the night. Perhaps, and probably, it was just that such a thing was never done. There are no traces of habitation here, only cultivation, and the mill, and, beyond the stream and on the far side of the beach, a sheepfold that was, at that time, still used. But not today.

The islanders, on the whole, do not seem to relish being on the island alone. In lambing time they come together, on a few widely spaced-out days, but no one comes to live as a solitary shepherd to take care of the sheep every day at this tricky season. Consequently many sheep and lambs are lost from neglect (We manage these things better in Yorkshire). Lately an English family on holiday in May saved a lamb, whose mother died after giving birth, by feeding it from a bottle. They brought the bottle to the island after having seen lambs die in previous years. When the crofters came over they claimed the lamb, and took it away to rear. Then these part-time islanders found another lamb starving beside its dead mother, and this one also they bottle-fed. But the crofters did not come again. So the pet-lamb was transported, on the insistence of the children, back to a Midland garden. There it thrived, graduated to eating lawns, marigolds and privet-hedges, and was eventually put in the care of a local farmer, with instructions not to slaughter. So there is a Hebridean sheep somewhere among the plump Sassenach sheep of Midland England. Even the sheep migrate.

But here I still stand on the edge of the amphitheatre of tumbled boulders that is Moil Mor beach. The millstream has gurgled away underneath the stones and emerged lower down on a sandier part of the shore. Beyond lie more weedy boulders, and a small offshore island that is possible to reach at low tide, but is cut off at high tide. One has to be fairly agile to reach it at any time, as its sides are sheer and slippery, and once on it there are nightmare cracks through which one can peer down at waves that surge in underneath this island, designed for the happiness and safety of otters rather than people and their sheep. Very few of the latter reach this island, so the sea-thrift grows un-nibbled into a turf of great green warts, and the wild angelica grows tall in late Summer, and erects its nodding white umbrellas unmutilated by the grazing breed that cuts everything down to size.

But the most remarkable thing about this beach is that it seems to be the local litter-bin for the Atlantic. When we lived in the blackhouse, and before we had learned its real name, we used to call it the driftwood beach, for it is piled with logs, planks, and pieces of broken boats and boxes, as though it were the haunt of wreckers. And of course the bay stretches its wide arms out directly towards the South-west, and the Southwest wind is a wrecker. Moil Mor beach picks up the pieces, and once they are high on the steep bank of boulders there they stay. Bigger waves than the ones that brought them in would only shove them further up the beach.

Here are broken hulls, rusty ship's boilers, empty barrels, open fishboxes, rudders, whole planks from cargoes of timber, plastic bottles of various shapes and sizes, oildrums, broken toys, toothless and gaping boots, tangles of rope, bright coloured plastic and grey aluminium floats, fishnets, kreels, hawsers like dead pythons, a packingcase with Russian writing on it, a sodden hairy coconut, a part of a derrick with a rusting hook, and, most conspicuously, huge salt-white logs that have, presumably, escaped from logjams and swum the ocean currents from the East coast of Canada. These lie piled randomly together, crisscrossed like matchsticks round the rim of a vast ashtray.

Barked, and sanded smooth by rough treatment, with worn stumps where once their amputated branches grew, some of these tree-corpses are riddled with large holes that suggest an unpleasantly large variety of sea-woodworm; others are fairly sound. Some are small enough to be dragged home and sawn up for the fire, others are impossibly large.

74

In the old days the islanders would never have seen trees of half the size that these dismembered torsos suggest.

The only tree that is really designed to grow on Scarp is Juniper Horizontalis. This creeps about, in its unambitious manner, close to the ground of the very crown of Strone Romul. There are Rowans, sheared by the wind, on some islands in the tarn, and a stunted Sycamore dying in the old Post Office garden. Also, there are in the village several little plantations of Willows, sheltered from sheep by encircling walls, which were probably for the purpose of making lobster kreels and peat-baskets in the old days. Apart from this list, Scarp can fairly be described as treeless, though it need not be in the sheltered places, but for sheep.

While on Scarp, a visit to Moil Mor is comparable to a visit to the Oxfam Shop in town. One never knows what nearly-free bargains may be found. Inexplicable lumps of paraffin wax for lighting the fire, or making candles; the bones of seals for those studying biology; and even, once, a waxy mass of yellowish substance that we took at first for beeswax, but which proved to be ambergris — supposedly worth hundreds of pounds. After a stormy Winter almost anything may turn up. We come to sift through the latest consignments of secondhand forest, and the charitable sea's deliveries of the rich world's leavings, and are comforted mainly by the proof, manifest in driftings from the tropics and the antipodes, that we are not alone and the sundered world is, in fact, one world.

Waves

Here, this morning, no wind gave warning;
the tall and roaring waves simply arrived.
They ride like a dark blue army with white plumes.
Their impulse was in mid-ocean, days ago:
and the impulse behind the impulse? and who gave orders?
Who filled in and signed the forms?

What a charge it is! What a charge it must have been
that such a weight of water be lifted and thrown
again and again by causes unknown.
What inequities provoked this swell of rage?

The sound is bridged by breakers –
green over sandbar shallows, snarling with foam
till, darkening, they reform themselves, to rush
towards our rocks and explode.
Our small white boat is threatened.

Not only the obvious waves, the less obvious rock
is anchored in other times, and in other places.
Not only no man, but no island is truly an island;
Earth is one mainland home
where ancient roots are meshed
like seaweed tangles dredged up by the storm.

A Fank

As we are clearing away our breakfast the growing hum of an outboard emerges from the silence outside. A boat slides into sight round the rocks, with a conspiracy of crofters crowded into it. Then we notice that a gathering of battered vans and cars has come to rest on the other side of the sound, by Husinish pier, and another cluster of tiny, distant men is embarking in a second boat. Soon its engine, also, becomes audible, while the first boat is being hauled up Scarp's slipway, and the crofters unload their lunches, coats, cans of poisonous dip, clipping-shears, and so on; and their dogs unload themselves. The second boat glides round the point, also carrying an earnest conference of philosophers on board. It too unloads its men, dogs and gear, and suddenly the island is crowded. Men and dogs scatter about the hillside, appearing on every ridge and headland. A group fills up the sheep-dipping trough, down by the shore, by means of a long snake of plastic hose running from Margaret McInnes' old but unfailing tap: others set off purposefully to round up their sheep and lambs from the crags.

We should have expected this, for yesterday much shouting, barking and bleating from Cravadale, on the other side, told us that a fank was in progress over there; and this is the way it goes. First they attend to the sheep on that side, and then on this; for most local crofters have sheep and grazing-rights on both sides of the sound.

In the old days fanks were much more like picnics. Women and girls also took part, walking over the island with the day's food and a big kettle for brewing tea, while the men ran round and about the island. Fanks encompassed both business and pleasure, and many a courtship began or progressed at the fank, where the women would serve tea to the men who had run round the island to fetch the sheep, then have tea themselves before helping with the sheep. The work of clipping and dosing for fluke would be done close by the sheepfold at Moil Mor; the water for tea was fetched from the burn there, and boiled on a campfire of driftwood from the beach. Later the lambs, separated from their mothers, would be brought round the coast to be ferried to Fladday, a low green island about half a mile away. Thus the lambs were weaned, and the untouched flowery turf of Fladday, where the terns had just finished nesting, would be transformed to living mutton. These days the clipping is done in the fold down by the dip, for there is no longer any reason why the sheep should not

77

be allowed back inside the village fence in high Summer, for no-one has any crops to be kept inviolate from the nibblers.

Nowadays no women come over to the fank, and the old men stay by the sheepfold to prepare the dip and to make the tea; and to talk.

Another Angus, a smaller and stockier man, (and a cousin of big Angus) who, though born on Scarp, has lived much of his life on the mainland, talks to us about the old times. Of big Angus he says – "I miss him; Oh how I miss him!" with deep sighs. Then he points out a tiny, distant house, all alone on the hillside above Loch Cravadale. "I lived there for eighteen years. I and my wife had five children there. I was the salmon-watcher. They were the best years."

He lives now in one of the group of cottages that are gathered in the shade of the laird's castle, five miles away.

He tells us how the new landlords at the castle like their lobsters to be served. He talks about the catching and cooking of salmon. And of its eating. Then he embarks on an anecdote of the old days on Scarp.

A man was walking alone by the shore at Moil Mor. He startled an otter, which ran under a rock; but the man made a rush and grabbed the otter by its tail and pulled it from under the rock. He swung it by the tail, over his shoulder, intending to swing it back and dash out its brains on the rock. For he wanted its pelt. But the otter got its teeth into the seat of the man's trousers, and wouldn't let go. So the man held the otter fast by the tail, and the otter held the man fast by the seat of the trousers, and the man set off up and over the mountain, all the way home with the otter at his back. Once in his house he called to his wife: 'Look you, Wife,' he said, 'will you fetch the poker or the tongs and give this otter that has me by the trousers a really sharp crack on the head. Then we can sell its pelt.' The wife fetched the tongs and took a good swing and gave her husband a really hard crack on the backside. The man gave a great shout and let go of the otter's tail, whereupon the otter let go of the man's trousers and escaped, running to the sea.

Angus seems to be as pleased as we are that the otter should have had the best of it; but the sheep can now be heard, like a disorderly army coming round by the south shore towards the fank. The dogs bark, the men shout, and the undisciplined rabble of sheep approach, bleating in protest.

We leave Angus to the serious business of dipping sheep.

It cannot be denied that these croftings occasions are labour-intensive. Though the sheep are herded by all, each man clips and doses his own property. The dipping has to be done collectively, but

78

any trimming of horns or dabbing of identifying colours onto the sheep is done by each man for his own. The whole Scarp flock together is no larger than that of one farmer in Yorkshire, yet about fifteen men, each with a dog, turn out to a fank. The men co-operate well, but so many dogs create muddle. Consignments of sheep, when they realise that they are in for a sea journey, frequently succeed in escaping from the cordon of dogs and men, and have to be rounded up all over again. Much strenuous running about is called for, up and down stony hillsides. The dogs bark and contradict each other. The sheep become more than usually confused. I think of our neighbour in Yorkshire: he, his son, and one thought-reading dog, gather and enfold more than a hundred sheep with no fuss, no shouting, but merely a few whistles. One year a man who was born on Scarp, but has worked as a shepherd in the lowlands for thirty years, was full of ideas for improvement. He would construct a permanent fence along here – to keep the sheep from running about the hill: he would use a surplus army landing-craft for taking the sheep over the waters and so on. Naturally, nobody wanted to hear him. In Scarp things are done in the time-honoured way, and changes are not looked for.

This year, though, the men are nearly all wearing plastic over-trousers. This is an innovation. It always used to be wellingtons or waders, which filled up with water long before the end of the ferrying operation. So changes can happen.

Like devils loading sinful souls into the boat for Hell, the crofters carry the sheep to the boat and pack them in between and below the seats. They put in as many as possible for each journey, so they cannot move, though they seem to understand the folly of jumping overboard. When the boats are full they push off from the jetty and putter gently over the calm water. The previous boat may already be on its way back. When it arrives, empty, more resigned sheep are detached from the dense crowd which is kept together by a few yards of netting fence, held about them by men serving as fencing posts, and dragged like living sacks towards the boat where the packing of sinful souls goes on.

Meanwhile, in the distance, the other boat has arrived at Fladday and the small pale maggot-shapes of sheep can be seen, fanning out over the beautiful turf as they are put ashore. The penitent souls are relieved to find they have arrived in Heaven instead of Hell, and they crop the grass gratefully. It will be less heavenly by October, when they are brought back to Scarp for the Winter. And Scarp itself can barely support them: all the sheep will be very hungry by the Spring. In Yorkshire they would be fed – on hay – but here both men and beasts live on stony ground, and that means poverty. And poverty means no Winter feed for the sheep.

Yet there are fish in the sea. Can the depth of the sea not atone for the shallowness of the soil? Could this place not be as wealthy as Yorkshire? Islands like Scarp could be one farm. Their steep hillsides could be terraced. Might they not grow soft-fruit, and have a small jam-factory and fish-cannery? There could be several full-time weavers; a windcharger for electricity; a better harbour, for a trawler or a couple of lobster boats. A helicopter dental service, every three months, perhaps. My imagination repopulates the island in preparation for the twenty-first century, as the crofter boats shuttle to and fro until all the sheep are at last transported.

Taking their excess of dogs, and a few helpless sheep with front legs tied to back legs, trussed for slaughter, the crofters leave the island empty but for ourselves. The sound of their engines diminishes into the silence of the evening, but we can still hear, from across the water, the calling of middle-aged lambs on Fladday. They have not yet forgotten their mothers, who bleat back to them from the hillsides of Scarp.

Scarp Song

My two strong sons skate out in one small shoe
      treading the polished water
across inverted hills that hang stone heads
among the white clouds in its green glass mirror.

The wind sleeps, and a blanket mist may thicken,
      hiding the polished water,
and no one knows which breathing wind may cloud
the glass, and frost or shiver the green mirror.

All my love's work sits in that far white boat,
      trusting the smiling traitor,
diminishes beyond duststorms of birds.
I see long threads of white hair in the mirror.

My sons ride fearlessly, far out to sea;
      I would not have them other:
they cheat the traitor of his mackerel shoal
and teach the lobster to repent his error.

Northeaster, chase them home; bring rainbow weather
      across the ruffled water.
Confine, Southwest, remorseless water-walls
that travel blind. I dare not name my terror.

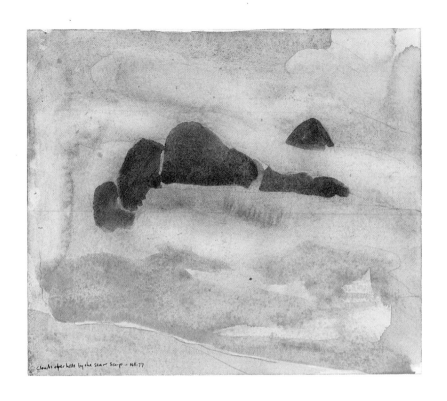

Clouds over hills by the sea — Scarp

Analysis of the Silence

This silence is lack of telephone-bells and traffic,
absence of feet through grass or keels through waves,
the gagging of rumour, or radio-voice and static,

and presence of shrill wren-signals, gannet-dives –
their splash, emergence, wing-claps of self-applause –
and sighs of pale, bottle-glass green sea that heaves

its sandbank mattress over: small motors of bees
that hum low over the ground: furtive crumble of walls,
and secret mitosis of cells in leaves: far cries

of squealing terns, discordant as unoiled wheels
above the deafening roar in the hub of the world's
invisible dynamo thundering here, that feels

like silence. But here, where deft gannets pin chiffon folds
of water scarves, I can hear, under all, the terrific
engines. Here is the axle-tree that holds

the planet in place, and controls the unsleeping traffic.

To Kearstay Beach

We first saw this beach in 1969. We looked down from the edge of the island just below the peak of Strone Romul. We were walking right round the island on a heatwave day, scrambling over the pathless rocks and wading through kneedeep heather, and in our sweaty state, and after our dry corned beef sandwiches, the white sand under its washes of sea-green water looked like an inaccessible heaven.

Today, eight years later, is the day that we shall actually go there. A light north-east wind blows, and the sun shines out of a flawless sky onto blue water as we carry our drawing gear, bathing towels and sandwiches down to the jetty. There we are stopped in our tracks by the dark shape of a mink caught off its guard, sunning itself. It doesn't run away at once, but peers at us curiously; so we have the opportunity to stare back. It is a very pretty little predator − long, lithe body, round ears, round eyes and pointed nose. Smaller than a cat. It withdraws its sinuous darkness into the shadows under the old roadway that has been broken up by the sea, and we continue down the jetty. The boys row out in the dinghy and bring the boat in from its mooring. We are going to tow the dinghy behind us, and it is already trailing from the boat's stern where we clamp the powerful but under-exercised Johnson engine. Our gear is stowed, we are aboard, and the boys cast off and step aboard also. We row out into the fresh breeze, while the engine takes a great many pulls to get started. At last it coughs and grumbles into action and we are off northward, along the coast.

Passing familiar sheepfolds and loops of stone wall that once contained gardens, we can see clearly the pattern of the old cultivation ridges scarring the shore. Generations of backbending have left an indelible mark, but though I appreciate how much hard work went into making all these hillside shelves upon which crops were supported, the crofters have so nearly terraced the steep in the Mediterranean manner that it seems a shame that they couldn't have toiled just that much harder, and more co-operatively, so that the whole hillside could be tamed and bound about with continuous horizontals. True, the stone is granite; true, the soil is sparse and, in many places, boggy; but if so much could have been done, then it could all have been done. The necessary manure lies ever-renewing itself as seaweed on the shore below, and this hillside is no steeper than many an Italian hill. But it is useless to wish it terraced and productive; it is intermittently scarred and productive of nothing but grass, wild flowers and nests of the meadow-pipits that are Scarp's sparrows. There is no trace of the crests of bluish-green oats that used to wave and sigh here at this season, nor even of the corn-marigolds that bloomed like garden flowers on the ridges where oats or rye had been a year or two previously. A few sheep, naked and pale from recent shearing, and bigbellied because big bellies are an occupational hazard of herbivores, cluster together to devastate the botany. I know well what it consists of – devilsbit, tormentil, centaury, field gentian, bog-saxifrage, bog asphodel, a little knapweed and some stunted ragwort. The orchid season is already over.

Beyond the village fence there are no cultivation scars. The turf is entirely heather, with small closecropped, grassy patches, boulders, and ever-increasing crags. A burn cuts a track through the heather and falls from the cliff edge at Geo Forse where the cliff hangs out over the sea and the fulmars nest on the ledges. They fly about their cliff like a midge-swarm. On a jutting rock that slopes towards the water what appears at first to be a broken fence of short irregular stakes proves to be a group of perching shags. They see us coming, and some of them dive, streamlined, into the water, making no splash. A cormorant surfaces near our boat, and disappears again hastily. Black guillemots leave the water and fly off, heavy-bellied and reminiscent of bumblebees with their whirring wings. Some actual bumblebees go humming past like bullets, drawn across the water by the scent of heather. The heather clings to north Scarp's extraordinary landscape of crag beyond the crag – a wilderness untameable by man. Useless to think of terraces here. Well may the Vikings have called it 'Scarp', and departed.

Behind us now, the shags, back on their rock, are extending their wings to dry them in the sun.

Ahead lies the point of Slettnish, further than which we have never been by boat. A steep, open funnel of heather and rock slopes from between two peaks, down to sea-level. Here, at times, the eagles can be seen playing in the rising air, but I have never seen them. Beyond Slettnish and its scattered rocks, which necessitate a wide detour, far from the shore, we meet the swell from the North Atlantic. The tide is full, and some of the rocks are only white warnings of broken water. We give them all a wide berth and see what must be the east end of Kearstay island, just showing. Then we curve round westward into Kearstay sound.

The white beach is still far away, across the deep waters, but the scene looks like a huge stageset. There is the white strip of sand, the blue-green of shallow water between Scarp and its infant island, and

85

the high overhanging cliff of reddish granite, gnarled and knotted with congealed boilings of molten rock. The cliff leans over deep green water, and on this water a blue-painted lobster boat lies at anchor, looking like a miniature pirate ship. It shows no signs of life: it could be the Marie-Celeste, unaccountably deserted, or its crew may be asleep below. We do not disturb it but pass on towards the beach.

The fulmars fly curiously about our boat as we hum gently through the sound, peering overboard into the water to make sure of a patch of sand on which to drop the anchor. We don't approach too close to the beach for fear that the receding tide may leave us high and dry, so we anchor about a hundred yards from the shore, and row the dinghy in.

So here we are at last. It has taken us eight years to get here, but the same sun shines round the western shoulder of the mountain onto the beach; the same kingfisher-coloured sea washes between Kearstay and Scarp. The descendants of the same fulmars whirl about their cliff, and what may be the same eagle soars up into the sun-dazzle and rises higher and higher, till, as small as a dust-speck, it draws a vast arc towards the Harris mainland.

The receding tide leaves vivid-coloured detritus at the high water-mark. A coral-coloured crab-back, a mauvey-blue lobster-claw, small pink shells such as we used to call 'angel's toenails'; a bright green scrap of weed. Dazzled by the white beach, the eye takes refuge in such fragmentary details. The sand bears no human prints, but otter and smaller, starry mink tracks abound. In and out of the water – to and fro between adjacent caves – deep into the cool darkness of rocky folds and creases. Gambolling along the tideline.

We haul up the dinghy and take stock of our new territory.

The beach tilts steeply to deep water at high tide. At the west end of the beach a nine-foot wall of sand stands like a miniature cliff or a very tall step. The stream that descends in fall after fall from the crags, at first winds about in a deep bed carved in the sand, then fans out into a wide shallow river to the sea. To the East – red cliffs leaning over deep water, beyond the caves. To the West – a grassy slope and rocky knoll, beyond the stream. This is all, but for the green island across the dazzling sound where a bridging sandbank begins to emerge as the tide goes down. And the hollow sky where the eagle disappeared: and the screaming fulmars.

I walk over the closecropped granite knoll to the west. Still dazzled I look downward at short-stemmed devilsbit, crawling tormentil, tufts of thrift, and sheep droppings. At the far side of the knoll the ground stops abruptly at a sheer drop. Beyond a dreadful fissure, floored by sea, is an island of broken rock, full of cracks, deep and vertical, with sea glinting in darkness far below. This is the fortress that defends the beach from the Atlantic. I can see where the most recent slabs of granite have been exploded away by Winter storms. The rock bears none of the yellow and grey lichen that covers the long-exposed surfaces.

Even today the Atlantic swell breaks on the westward headlands of Kearstay island. Zigzags of rock bear wavering white tongues of foam. Far out to sea the islets are smothered in foam about their rocky bases. Lobster boats cruise to and fro, drifting close to the rocks to pull up their kreels. Far bright floats gleam beside most of the glorigs and skerries.

The anchored ship under the red cliff still sleeps. There has been no sign of life from her. Nor is there any sign of life on Kearstay island, though I can see the smooth rocks, under a shadow-casting overhang, where a small colony of seals is said to breed. Offshore a multitude of fulmars drifts about like a flurry of squeaking snow. Then a redpainted lobster-boat hums round Slettnish point and turns towards Kearstay sound. It trails the antennae of its wake behind it, and slows up alongside the sleeping ship. Men spill over from the red ship to the blue, as in an act of piracy. Have they come to mend a broken-down engine? to deliver or collect gear? to pay a social call? It's none of my business; and, in any case, the boarding party returns shortly to its own red ship, which roars off proudly, leaving a shining wake.

This land where I sit bears signs of man. The scars are not as haphazard as on many lazybed sites, but the whole area, of about ten acres, is covered in parallel ridges. The rounded corrugations are clothed in a closecropped turf that has long forgotten oats, rye, barley or potatoes, if these were the crops they knew; for no one remembers the cultivation of this slope, and no one's father or grandfather can be remembered to have remembered, either. Or so we are told. The long mounds lie like the graves of giants, or like sibling caterpillars on the green leaf of the land. They could have been the inspiration for corrugated iron; or the nameless men of the old time could simply have been sculpting in soil a replica of the green swell of the sea.

Many parts of the island remind me of the faces of those primitive peoples who decorate their skins with an embroidery of ridged scars. One wonders if this is all man is: a pattern-maker. All that seems to be left of him when he goes are the patterns of a creature with a preference for straight lines and right-angles, who therefore makes a rectangular nest. But I refuse to believe that this is so. We are more than the marks we make; even those marks on paper that I am so addicted to. We are also more than our fine speeches, and one or two memorable deeds. For, even supposing the whole earth were to become like Scarp – scarred with the geometrical tracks of an extinct creature – the pattern-makers, whose patterns are only a residue of what they were actually engaged in, would still have made those strange inner beings that are ourselves; that feed on speech and song, and are enriched by giving. And though no one might then understand that these things had been, yet they are not to be denied; for we have taken possession of our scrap of eternity: and here we shall stay, whatever may crumble.

While we draw, eat our lunch, and explore, the sea recedes, and we swim in the pale green water of low tide. The sunlight shining through the clear water is transformed to ribbons of rainbow light on the white sand floor of the sea. I have never noticed this before. My every movement makes the rainbows undulate. A shoal of sand-eels riddles the water between me and the seabed, casting clear shadows on the white sand, among the rainbows. A portion of sand removes itself from the rainbow-strewn floor, and a flounder flaps away. I could swim in this liquid light forever, but I do not wish to become too cold for the homeward journey. So I emerge and dress.

On the way back the sea is silkily calm. The rocks of Slettnish now jut clear out of the water. The cormorants perched on the nearest one take flight together as we pass. They fly low, close to the water. Further on we stop to pull up our lobster-pots, which contain no lobsters but two edible crabs and one white-bellied, leopard-spotted, sandpaper-skinned dogfish. I would cheerfully fling this back, but the boys like to make meals from the horrors of the deep. This creature has lidded eyes, like a lizard's, that make it appear to have more than a round-eyed fishy intelligence. The gritty roughness of its skin is really an extension of its teeth: its custom is to wrap round its prey and crush it. Its actual teeth are very sharp, and – the islanders tell us – it has a very dirty bite. People have been known to die of bloodpoisoning after being bitten. So we are told. So we don't attempt to remove it from the kreel while still in the boat. We have also caught, among the small-fry of nonentities that will creep into lobster pots, a small and lively crab whose name is unknown to me. It is very quick and purposeful in its movements, and has a saw-edged front to its shell, vermilion-jointed legs, tiger-stripes on legs and claws, and scarlet beads for eyes. I am trying to release it from the kreel and throw it back into the sea, but though so lively, and seemingly full of intelligence, it misunderstands my motives. It lashes about with its legs and clashes its claws together over the top of its shell, and draws blood. My blood. But it has wounded me without malice, since it lives in the world where things have no names and it speaks in the language of reflexes. I leave it to the mercy of the boys, who kill it first and handle it afterwards, as they do also with the dogfish.

Our sorting out of kreels and their contents is deferred when we first arrive back at Scarp's jetty. We are just clambering ashore and about to unload our gear when we hear shouts. Crofters have been here most of the day, tending sheep, and they are clipping and dipping still, over on the other side of the harbour. A panic-stricken sheep has run from the men and dogs and slipped from the rocks into the water. It swims aimlessly, and is rapidly leaving the shore behind. The crofters are shouting at us and pointing at the small, white drifting creature, dogpaddling ineffectually with cloven feet. It slides further and further into the current. We can, of course, get out to sea far quicker than the crofters with their heavy boats, which are not in readiness.

We push off from the jetty again, the engine starts obediently, and we make a well-calculated curve to head off the poor beast which is still swimming desperately – its head thrown back and its eyes staring. Jacob grabs it by the horns, and then around its body. He hauls it, dripping, on board, as though it were a kreel. I hold it fast lest it should wish to jump overboard, misunderstanding our good intentions; but it shows no signs of any such inclination. Its saturated fleece soaks me to the skin.

When we hand it over to the crofters on the rocks, they are laughing.

"Did you give it the kiss of life?" they ask.

"You should breed sheep with webbed feet," we answer.

At home the boys boil and dress the crabs; I cook vegetables and disguise the sea-monster. We go to bed very late, as usual, and very well, though eccentrically, fed.

Otter Letter

I knew you at first glance, though far offshore,
disporting in the satin-surfaced sea.
You were no seal – too small, and too alert –
you hadn't that forsaken-merman stare
with which seals look at land, as though a man
were bedded in that seamless blubber coat.
You hadn't their blunt, slablike look, but peered
inquisitively, with your pointed head
craning from feline shoulders, at the brash
and shouting perpendiculars that walked.
You looked amazed – amused –
at our impedimenta – rubber boats,
our oars and engines – where, just in your skin,
you're fearlessly, amphibiously, at home
and, I suspect, glad not to be a man.
You own the title deeds to rocks and caves:
you've signed the parchment beach. Your tracks confirm
possession. Here you landed, shook yourself
and scratched up sand, and rolled, then wrote along
the lines between obliterating waves
and last saliva splash of lapping tide.
This is an otter beach. Your kind belongs
to seas where we are poor forked aliens –
helpless without those cities at our backs
that make our adaptations to your world.
Insouciant as a cormorant, you dived –
I glimpsed your flank, which curved like a small wave –
and disappeared into your element.
Since then your streamlined joy possesses me,
and leads me on to write.
For all our lacks –
our insulating boots and plastic macs,
sea crutches, sea-bathchairs, and our false limbs –
we humans have some assets. Empathy.
We dive into mind's all-reflecting sea
for images, and words that leave live tracks.

Scarp Desolate

I can remember thinking, when the island community left, "Well, at least it will be good for the botany;" but this has not been so. The human race gives itself a bad press lately. We have taken to regarding ourselves as the blight of Earth; but I would like to defend us. In moderation we are very good for nature, and for landscape, but this opinion may be simply the result of the onset of middle age and deteriorating vision. Certainly I am no longer the romantic who used to like nothing better than a rip-roaring wilderness. I now like gardens. The world is just jungle and tangle and desolation without them. I even, sometimes, have a nostalgia for suburbs, but this is cured instantly, the moment I set foot in one. Nevertheless, I can now understand those islanders, marooned in the stone-age, with doctors and dentists miles away across seas and mountains, and whose life-long efforts could achieve only subsistence, craving the easier life of cities and suburbs, where nature is kept in place, and where there are possibilities to develop other talents than backbending. Scarp was scarcely the land of opportunity.

I thought, though, that it might become the land of opportunity for plants; but I was wrong. The botany is actually impoverished by the cessation of human habitation and cultivation, and – perhaps – by the absence of cows. There used to be certain fields that, during the years when they were left to lie fallow, grew a nodding crop of scarlet poppies beside the glittering sea. Other places grew corn-marigolds in such profusion that they seemed like a patch of sunlight in a clouded landscape. Heartsease also grew on fallow fields, and an ultramarine vetch scrambled about in the grass of hayfields. There were various sorts of large, yellow-centred, white daisies. These have all disappeared; only a remnant of the heartsease still remains, dwindling year by year. One reason for this is that certain plants like to have the soil turned over for them. They do not keep on reappearing in an undisturbed mat of turf. Another reason is that now that no one is cultivating, the sheep, which are still grazing Scarp's pasture, have things almost entirely their own way. There are no gardens to be protected, no hayfields to grow tall, so the sheep are pushed outside the village fence very late, and let in again in mid-August. So such flowers as primroses, persistently nibbled down until late June, only manage to flower in July and August. Harebells – and there used to be certain small fields and knolls that were blue with harebells in late August – are becoming a furtive and fugitive species. There are fewer early-purple, and white, and pink-spotted orchids. The bog-asphodel thrives because it is poisonous, and the thistle because it is prickly; but most of the gentle and harmless are knuckling under. Swamp flowers such as kingcups and ragged-robin survive, and the annual field-gentian and centaury still carpet the clifftops; but the dark cities of the burdock are usually nibbled to ruins before they are completely built, and the wild angelica seldom grows tall, or erects its greenish-white umbrellas unmutilated. The wild carrot, which I suspect to be poisonous, usurps much of the machair that used to be a rich mixture of clovers, vetch, harebells and knapweed; and even the noxious ragwort never grows into fullsize plants, but flowers six inches from the ground.

The archetypal Scotch thistle is not really better off than it was under the dominion of man, because it really likes broken ground. These tall and magnificent biennials grow inside houses where the roofs have fallen, on the banks of streams or by the shore where there has been some erosion. The most successful thistle is a miserable, small-flowered, straggly runt that grows in great communal patches. And, of course, the nettle thrives.

For two or three years corncrakes called, like unanswered telephones, from the hearts of the dark nettle-forests; but these have now fallen silent and disappeared, probably prey to the interloping mink which multiply unchecked. Humans are at fault for introducing these versatile predators, and they are at fault in covering the land with sheep. Without the latter there would be more honeysuckle, more briar-rose thickets, more willow trees and more rowans. Certain round-leaved poplars would climb down from the inaccessible crags where they cling on for dear life, and a low forest of windbent trees would develop. But without man the weeds of cultivation would still be missing, as would the cultivated plants themselves. Oats, rye, barley and potatoes are also botany, and also beautiful. And one of the beautiful things about them is that they grow at the behest of people, beneath untameable crags and beside untrustworthy seas, enclosed in the bright geometry of fields.

Depopulation Play, Set on the Island of Scarp, With a Cast of No One

The scenery is well enough,
but what about the actors? What indeed?
The heroine grew old,
remembered everything except her lines
and died. The heroes left –
renouncing crowns and titles – long ago,
and went to Glasgow. Only clowns remained
to play to empty houses:
houses once full of laughter, silent now,
or full of scornful birds.
Exits were made in weeping groups, by boat,
not drawn by swans but driven by machines
leaving an oily wake, to no applause.
And no one volunteered for Crusoe's part
except for amateurs, who soon gave up
after a few brief seasons, but –
compelled – the show goes on.
Gauzes drift in, mad as Ophelia,
uncertain of their cues, and then dissolve.
The safety curtain falls and sticks half-way,
blots out the stage while scene-shifters wheel in
the same old rocks and mountains, then
rainbows and storms, lost properties,
a lobster-boat from a far-distant play,
some ships of fools, opposing winds,
alarums and excursions, silences.
A squall sets waves to smiling false white smiles;
the beach is strewn with wigs
and litter hurled ashore by hissing seas.
The script is wordless, may be meaningless,
by poltergeists, or by the Lighting Man.
The drama is of light. Topping the bill
are tightrope-walking Sun, Trapezing Moon.
The sea itself changes its coloured lights,
gives Winter matinees, and plays all night
to choruses of stars.

A Departure

Probably we left our 1977 departure a little late. We had named August 31st as the day for our leaving, September and the equinox being a notoriously unsettled time. Then great South-westers push the entire force of the Atlantic swell into Scarp's narrow sound, and even a strong North-wester can wrap the island round in warring waves. And – "The better the weather has been in the Summer, the worse it is likely to be in the Autumn," says Joann, the widow of Angus McLennan, who sold us our home, "it will balance out." In Summer, everyone tells us, the sea may get up, but will go down in a day or two, but in Winter it may not go down for weeks.

Would this matter? If we were staying through the winter we wouldn't be anxiously watching the sea and the wind-direction each day, or lying awake at night listening to the sea roaring like a passing train, and the wind whining at the house-corners and rattling the slates on the roof. The weather had broken on the day following our visit to Kearstay beach. If we were staying on we would be cheerfully lifting our potatoes and storing them for the winter. We would be salting down the mackerel; for this is the season for shoals of those tiger-striped torpedoes of protein. "The sea has been boiling with mackerel in West Loch Tarbert," Joann said when we visited her in her exiled islander's council house, when we were over on a shopping trip.

"We used to clean the fish," she said, "and bone it, and put a layer of opened-out fish into a zinc bath, then a good layer of salt, then more fish, and so on until the bath was full; then cover it over. It must be well covered. This was very good in the Winter. Better than the frozen food."

If we were proper islanders, if we were staying, there would be oats to harvest, and grass to cut, dry and store for the cattle in Winter. Sometimes, in the old days, it was put into lofts in the byres, and sometimes it was left in little stacks, not much bigger than haycocks, in the open. It had to be covered with a snood of old fishing-net – bright orange or sea blue-green – and roped and pegged down well to keep it from the wind.

That, if we were not mere fly-by-nights, is what we would have been doing in late August and early September, rather than watching the sea and the ominous windy streaks in the evening sky, and trying to lull ourselves into security by saying "It's not September yet." We would be preparing for the great darkness of a Hebridean Winter, but instead we must leave with our harvest of art to tackle the market-places of the world.

★

Our last neighbour, the owner of the bungalow, had already had difficulty in leaving. He had only come for a few days to tidy his house up after the succession of families who inhabit it for a fortnight at a time through July and August. From the heart of England, by remote control, he had tried unsuccessfully to get a Harris plumber to come and clear the pipes which had stopped up during the sojourn of the family before the family before the last, so that the bungalow had reverted to such primitive forms of sanitation as most of us practise; and their baths had been in a basin in front of the kitchen fire. Having dug up his pipes and made some improvements to his hot water system, as well as having swum and fished, he appointed a day – the 25th – on which to leave. But that day, at dawn, the sky was pink and orange as though it was on fire. Beautiful but ominous. On the previous day the weather had been faltering in its perfection. From the top of the hill behind the village, in the evening, the visibility was very dim beyond the scaly old crocodile head of Husinish point. Low cloud shadowed Taransay and smudged Gaisker. There was no definite horizon, the green-grey sea became violet-grey at an indeterminate level, and the brightest thing in sea and sky was the snarl of white fangs at the tip of the crocodile snout, where the sea broke over the point. The boys brought in no fish that evening, either, and they came early saying the sea was more turbulent than it looked, and, once out on the water, the wind stronger.

★

By the time we got up on the morning of the 25th, the sea was full of sets of grinning teeth that appeared, disappeared and reappeared on the white and grey waves that travelled obliquely down the sound. The wind outside was strong enough to lean on, and formidable to walk against. At low water the boys walked northward up the shore, to see if they could see any sign of a kreel they had lost a day or two earlier, because its rope had broken. But they could see nothing of it, though the tide was very low, and acres of whispering brown weed were exposed. The sea would have broken it to pieces, anyway, for the short steep waves were hammering at the shore, and rocking our moored boat like a seesaw. It had obviously had a very rough night,

95

and sat very low in the water, having taken a lot of sea on board. It was still having a very rough day, but there was nothing we could do for it until the gale abated and the sea went down. We had a philosophical discussion about whether it would be better off with or without its bung in, but practical activity was impossible. Our neighbour loitered about the jetty, watching the sea. Waves were falling downstairs towards the shore as though an escalator were having a nervous breakdown, frothing at the joints between treads and risers. He could see no way to persuade his boat to climb this unstable staircase onto the sea, and even if he could, he would then have to cope with a very fast and choppy sea and a force nine wind. His departure was not possible. So we invited him to supper that evening and we all found other things to do till then. I had discovered a new source of weather reports on Radio 2. This involved risking some minutes of alien music, but it was worthwhile to afflict the ears a little in order to catch its gale warnings, as it seemed to be the only station that realised that there were such things as fishermen or offshore islands, or any life at all beyond the suburbs of cities.

At midday I heard – "Attention all shipping. Here is a gale warning. Rockall, Hebrides and the Minches. North Easterly Gale, Force Nine. I will repeat that – " It was not news to us that the wind was blowing, but it was comforting to know that someone else knew about it. It was also comforting to know that while we could do little else but sit out the duration of the wind's ravings, the life of cities continued. The Edinburgh Festival was in progress, the arts of man were yet alive and the new dark age affected us alone. And we, though making a full-time job of survival, were able to listen to Carmen from Edinburgh that afternoon.

★

"Gale, force eight; moderating, backing northerly force five or six;" said the late night inshore waters forecast that evening. We all hoped that our neighbour's departure would be possible next day, and went to bed full of optimism.

Next morning, after looking at the sea and thinking better of it at about nine, he did eventually get away at about eleven-thirty, at low water, when the wind and sea quietened a little. He tied himself to his boat, while his large golden Labrador sat calmly beside the stowed luggage, and he set off due North-West, almost straight at the oncoming waves, then turned to approach them more obliquely until very nearly across to the beach to the Eastward, when he coasted

96

down along the shore of Harris in the shelter of the black cliffs where the cormorants are at home. The undulations of his boat seemed quite considerable, even over there. We watched him through binoculars until we lost sight of him among the corrugations of rougher water along the Husinish shore; but we did eventually see what appeared to be a very small and wet person creep ashore up the jetty, and go to-and-fro with bags and packages, loading his car. So we knew he was alright, and, also, that we were alone.

I went to the beach. The tide was very low, but the scrubbed withdrawing room of the sea was strewn with swags of weed: long ribbons with claw roots still gripping their dislodged seabed stones; great goffered frills and ruffs of weed; spiral convolutions of brown rubber. Though beaches have happy associations – of childhood, summer holidays, our own parents, irresponsibility and play – they are really very melancholy places. The sea is the earth's arch-nihilist. Human values are unknown to it. No-one can take art seriously on a beach, for nothing prevails here except appetite, and the reiteration of "Smash – smash – smash," which mocks our desire to make some permanent mark, to erect a permanent structure, or to survive as an individual in any kind of permanent form. Survival here is by numbers – shoals of sand-eels or mackerel, the ever-hovering dust-storm of distant gannets, tangling their flightpaths in a collective rising, hovering and diving that forms a bridge over the dark sea. On such a rockstrewn beach, at Summer's end, one looks with dismay at the villages of limpets as though one were Poor Tom, the forked worm of King Lear's perceptive madness, and wonders how man can survive at all on this planet. For we are the Grasshoppers who have played all Summer long, and now the long Winter of want is upon us. The old islanders were the Ants. They lived in the cycle of the seasons, but we are, of necessity, fly-by-nights.

I moved along to the graveyard to cheer myself up.

This is a mound between a beach of granite boulders on one side, and, inland, the sheltered valley which lies before the old Post Office house, which still has its disused red telephone-box standing beside it. Through the valley runs a small burn, crossed by several broken planks and stone-slab bridges. This stream rustles and whispers through a dense plantation of flat-bladed iris swords. Before the gravemound the stream disappears into sandy ground, and must enter the sea invisibly, trickling under the piled granite eggs of the beach. The gravemound itself looks artificial, and is studded with these same egglike seashore boulders, one at the foot and one at the head of every inmate, for these are the islander's usual gravestones. It appears as

97

though layer on layer of dead people have been buried here, to form this unexpected mound; or as though the earliest dead had been buried inside the walls of an ancient broch: then, when the ground was full another layer had been started. Coffins, sand, coffins, sand, until the top layer of boulder-studded turf overtopped the encircling wall, which crumbled downward as the bonepacked earth rose up inside.

The graveyard is surrounded by a wire fence which does not keep the sheep out, so the grass is closely and tidily cropped. One enters by a ringing iron gate. Immediately beside the gate are Margaret and Angus MacInnes, and a step or two away, Angus MacLennan. Up the slope a little lies the postmaster who welcomed us, and gave sweets to the children, when we first came here in 1963. There are not many graveyards where I have so wide an acquaintance.

There are several conventional, mason-cut stones among the boulders, but I cannot find any named stones with dates earlier than 1900, though some broken slates may at one time have borne names now obliterated. There may have been some wooden headboards that bore names, but this is unlikely. Wood must always have been expensive on Scarp; it is hardly a local product. There is no tree of any size visible in the landscape for miles – throughout the long vistas of Lewis to the north, and South Harris and the other islands to the south. Good driftwood would have been used for the purposes of the living. Granite boulders are the one really plentiful crop of the Scarp shore, and they could easily be spared for the dead. Any attempts at lettering would only have defaced their beautiful sea-polished surfaces, so the dead lie anonymously under the cropped turf, except for a few successful sons or daughters of the island who, when they returned for burial after their respectable careers as schoolteachers or ministers, could afford a proper, mainland style, lettered stone. Or prosperous emigrant children of islanders nowadays may buy their buried parents a stone, as, indeed, the sons and daughters of Margaret and Angus have done. A small party of men came to erect the stone one day this summer – 'In loving memory of our dear parents.'

From the few inscribed stones we can know the names of the many who lie under nameless boulders, for besides having only a few surnames between them the islanders rang the changes on very few christian names. Babies would be named after their grandparents. Generations of women could go Margaret, Morag, Margaret, Morag; and I suppose second daughters would be named after great-aunts, so the Margaret MacInneses in the burial ground must be legion.

The surnames are MacKay, MacKinnon, MacLennon, MacInnes, MacDonald and MacLeod; and Donald, John, Murdo, Angus and

Hebridean Study

Norman, Annie, Kathleen, Margaret and Morag are the main fore-names. There is one stone to a man called Grant. He was a Glasgow man who married a Scarp girl, and when he died, in 1970, he asked that he might be buried on Scarp where he had spent his happiest days; so his coffin was delivered and the Scarp men buried him. Then the widow ordered and sent up a headstone, and came herself to stay with relatives on the island, to see it erected. But a dock-strike of that time kept the stone from being unloaded during the widow's stay, so she had to go home to Glasgow unsatisfied. Later, the stone was released and the men of Scarp carried it on a wooden stretcher between them from the jetty to the gravemound where they inserted it in the sandy turf and cemented it into place, facing the sea. Then it was that a young girl who was staying with her auntie on the island, and watching from a distance, with me, said – "Is that all the men there are left on Scarp?" in a voice expressive of real shock. It was the first time it had come home to her. I think there were five, and Murdo, who was disabled, looking on and making the number up to six.

This girl remembered a Scarp wedding of only a few years before when there had been twenty or thirty men, and the community had not yet realised that, through its young who would not stay to replace the old who went to the graveyard, the island population was leaking away.

A photograph of the stone in position was taken and, eventually, sent to the widow in Glasgow. No doubt she has been to see it since. Bones and stones are the people of Scarp's last plantings. Bones in Winter and stones in Summer. Nearly every year, in our absence, there is a new burial in the graveyard of the deserted island, for one or two of the Scarp exiles die every Winter. The funeral may be on mainland Harris but the burial is here. A boatful of men, in their best, dark suits, with the coffin laid across the plank seat between them, bring the Scarp man home to the brimming graveyard. The ground is now so full that some have to lie buried at uncomfortably sloping angles, with feet higher than head, or so it appears, for an eternity of slipping downward, as though camping on an ill-chosen site. Last Winter Angus MacInnes was put in beside Margaret, and there are other disturbances in the turf, with traces of wreaths caked in sand, like a line of outsize buttons, down the centre of recent graves. This Summer a boatload of crofters and ex-crofters, including the MacInnes brothers, came and put up a lettered stone for Margaret and Angus – 'Our dear parents'. And though it is beside the iron gate it turns its back on visitors to face the sea, though the hump of the gravemound intervenes.

For all the gravestones face the sea, as though, even now, when there is nothing to lose, the sea is not altogether trusted; it has to be watched. On calmest Summer days white waves break over the sandbank at low tide, and in Winter the huge smooth boulders piled on the beach are rolled forward over the grass, then clawed back again. The whole beach shifts and rattles. Great breakers scour the sand from the lower beach to pile it elsewhere, then it is brought back in a friendlier season.

I returned along the beach, in the teeth of the wind, which had now somewhat abated. It was no longer a wind for leaning on, but the sea was still very choppy. "I suppose that those transient porcelain gnashers that appear and disappear on the dark sea-surface might be called the false teeth of the gale". I amuse myself with such jokes while the Welshmen go humming by to retrieve their lobster-pots from beside Fladday; the sea drenches their boat with white spray as they cut through the waves. An hour later they were coasting back on the breakers, black pots stacked in their stern. It looked very exhilarating, but I knew it to be very cold and wet, in spite of the vivid yellow and orange oilskins they wore. But the seaway was coming to life again. Lobster fishers were on the move as the sun flickered out and in, and then out again; and later that afternoon the rainbows began.

Our last few days were full of rainbows. They are a Hebridean crop that grows in unsettled seasons: a substitute for the colours of treechange in Autumn elsewhere where there are trees. They spring from sea or land to mature, blossom and die, leaving not so much as a ghost. There are no fallen rainbows to sweep up, only rivulets gurgling down the hillsides.

At first there were broken rainbows propping the clouds over Harris in the late afternoon. Then an incomplete stalk of colours pushed at the cloud-ceiling to the North East. It became a double stalk, and there was a hint of a rainbow root at what should be its arrival place, in mid-sound. Quite suddenly, as though switched on, these parts were completed as a double arch, very bright. Curving over dark green sea the vivid inner rainbow cast brilliant light within its semicircle. The outer band, beyond a greyish interval, was less bright, and had its colours in reverse order, with red and then orange inside, as though it were a reflection of the primary rainbow. The whole glided slowly southward with the rain, gradually fading. The navy-blue darkness of non-reflecting sea in the sound was already in the island's shadow as the sun went down. And later, after an orange sunset, a nearly full moon sailed clear of cloud over a glittering night sea.

★

It was becoming a family joke that weather reports were my 'fix'. Even though all seemed to be on the mend, and we trusted the promises of rainbows and sunset, I sat up to hear the inshore waters weather forecast, as I did every night towards the end. I like to do this. I enjoy the opportunity for solitude. I like to be the only person awake in a sleeping house, sitting very still by the light of a storm-lantern, or candle, and thinking of the vast night around us, and the great undulations of the tide, glittering under the moon. Norman would go off to bed, taking the tilley lamp with him to read by. Quite soon I would hear him turn it out because his eyes were becoming too tired to focus on print, so the crack of light round the door disappeared and the faint sigh of released pressure died away, and I was alone with my feeble lamp, listening to the wind outside, or the hissing sea, or to late news or religious programmes, for kicks; or perhaps I would read Gerard Manley Hopkins, or brush my salt-sticky hair.

It became a kind of vigil, and it began to seem to me that it was not altogether futile for a woman to sit up alone on a remote island and simply bear in mind a visionary map of the seas laving our coasts – all their creeks and headlands, reefs and skerries and lonely islands – and the fishermen riding out with their undulating lights going to and fro on the dark water. The voice of the B.B.C. drew the map for me, and I traced it round from the Solway Firth to Cape Wrath, including the Minches, and from Cape Wrath to the Tyne. Mallin, Hebrides, Rockall, Fair Isle, Cromartie, Tyne, Forties and Dogger, with reports from weather stations Machrihanish and Tiree; Stornaway, Lerwick, Sule Skerrie, Aberdeen Dyce and Lucas.

Although I have been there, and know it to be rather a prim town of woolshops and religious bookshops, with public buildings designed by architects who could not conceivably have earned a living in any town where there was much competition, the name of Stornoway still conjures up a romantic image in my mind, resembling nineteenth century Nantucket, according to Melville. Tiree I know of as a low-lying island of market gardens and much sunshine, a going concern with vigorous human communities. Lerwick is Edwin Muir and Mackay Brown to me, but it is the name of Sule Skerrie I find most evocative. I imagine a lonely island of rock out in the grey seas to the

102

east of Inverness, waveswept and without vegetation, but inhabited by reclining seals that suckle their young, and croon to them through the night: but which of them sends out the weather reports, I don't know. Nor do I know my geography very well, but am well aware that the sea is dark and deep, and there are men upon it, seeking their livelihoods and our breakfasts.

One thing puzzled me at Friday's midnight. Everywhere the wind was backing, moderating, dropping to force four, and Northerly. But for Sea Area Rockall there was a gale warning. Southerly – force eight.

"Rockall is a long way off; more than a hundred miles to the other side of the St. Kildas" I thought, all through that calm Saturday, when the boys went out for the lobster pots in the morning, and were fishing as usual in the evening. The sea was clear and transparent like old greenish glass, so different from the preceding days of ruffled opacity.

From the cairn on the height behind the village the sky was pearly grey to the westward. There was no wind at ground level, but there was wind visible in the sky. The clouds appeared to have been back-combed, wearing frizzy white hairstyles. To the south-east the clouds were pink, as though reflecting a healthy sunset, but to Westward was greyish confusion and disturbance. The morning weather forecast at eight a.m. had repeated the southerly gale-warning, and it was plain, from my vantage point, that something was brewing in the South West. But visibility was good, and the broken teeth of the St. Kildas were clearly visible on the horizon, looking sad and grey to an eye that had read their story. No doubt they are now full of cheerful, rocket-tracking extroverts in uniform, but this is not the same as being inhabited by families who make their living there, and have been at one with its soil, generation after generation, for a thousand years.

To southward were the irregular sawtoothed edges of islands lying horizontally in the sea, one behind the other, in ever fainter and dimmer greys. Beyond the foreground of Husinish was Taransay, which is almost stretched into two islands, like a dividing cell. Beyond Taransay was Ben Luskentyre, with Luskentyre sands gleaming at its foot. Further off lay the ribbon of white shell-sand of Scarista and Northton, then Toe Head completed the South West corner of Harris. Beyond South Harris lay the low profiles of Pabbay, Berneray, North Uist, South Uist, and islands beyond islands beyond islands.

In the immediate foreground a hooded crow rose suddenly out of the ground to meet a fellow crow who was flapping by, and they both flew off cawing harshly. Brought back to the here and now, I climbed down through the dusk of the shadow side of Scarp to our house, to light a driftwood fire and scrub some potatoes before our boat, visible as a white scrap in the far distance to the north-eastward, should head home and its too-successful occupants compel an evening of gutting fish by storm-lantern light on the jetty.

★

We were awakened in the small hours of Sunday morning by the clattering of tiles and the creaking of the house that flexed its frame as though it were a ship. The wind leapt upon the southern gable-end again and again, and our hollow walls hummed with vibrations. The roof-tiles sounded like a line of falling dominoes at each gust, as though something ran up the roof. The curtains had been tugged out of the open window and were flapping noisily, so I got up to lower the sash. Outside the sea roared beyond the steep fields, while the full moon, occasionally visible amid racing cloud, shed a grey light that seemed like dawn. I returned to bed to lie and listen, and worry. If we were to have to wait long before it would be possible to cross the sound, it would be necessary to ration out the food. We had three tins of milk, one bag of flour, five pounds of rice and one of margarine. We had dried dinners enough for a fortnight, sugar and tea in plenty, and also water, ad lib. We would not starve, only become frustrated. So I was rocked and shaken back to sleep by the wind, and woke to a wild wet day on which we all kept a compulsory Sabbath. "Southerly gales, veering south west, Force eight, with stronger gusts" said even Radio Four, which usually lives in a sheltered world full of civilised current events, sprinkled with innoccuous showers and bright intervals.

The south-west wind swept along with it a smoke of fine rain that wrapped all who ventured out, as I did, in an instant wet blanket. I was saturated by the time I had reached the sea's edge, which I only wished to watch, as it roared in from several directions at once onto the beach. Over the sandbanks thirty or forty gannets were flying together; so many that ten or twelve might dive onto the same spot for the same fish, so it was attacked by a firing squad rather than a sniper. The birds rose and fell like a schizophrenic yo-yo, drawing an invisible cat's cradle on the rainy air. A bit of wet meant nothing to them, obviously. As their aerial ballet drifted nearer I could appreciate the marvellous, flexible control of the birds as they dived, then burst from the water with silver fish in their beaks, if they were lucky. They sat on the water, shook the fish to the back of their throats, and swallowed. Swimming on the water they look very like a white, yellow and black goose, but they are more typically seen in flight. In rough weather they often fly very close along the shore, so their peroxide yellow heads and necks, and their black pinions like black gloves, can be clearly seen. They are surprisingly large. Ben, who collects skulls, has both a gannet and a heron skull, and the gannet is considerable larger.

Terns, also, were fluttering and diving in the rainswept sea, their few ounces of wing-power making easy headway against the gale.

Across the sound the sea exploded in white thunder against the cliffs. Driven by a south-wester, the swell rides straight up the sound to smash against the Harris shore at an angle of about 45 degrees. Then the waves ricochet with diminished power towards Scarp's eastern beaches. This moving of waves in two directions at once makes the water build unstable pyramids where the waves cross over each other; but the full effect of these has to be appreciated from a small boat down on water-level. The secondary swell broke on the beach at my feet, when it had meshed in with the other waves that wrap around the island from the North. Quite suddenly, when you think you know the pattern and rhythm of the sea, a great wave will rear up like a cobra, in an entirely unexpected quarter, and chase you across the beach with snakelike speed.

High tide had been at eight-thirty that morning. Before breakfast we moved our dinghy well up onto the grass, out of reach of the largest imaginable wave; but there was no possibility of rescuing the boat from its mooring. Once again we had missed our chance on a calm day because we had been refusing to admit that Summer was over. So we had to leave the boat, with misgivings, in the care of the Good Lord. It was, after all, the Sabbath. It was a Sabbath on which the elements howled discordant psalms of praise all day, and shut us into the house.

★

At midday on Monday a lone yachtsman appeared. At first we saw only a frail vertical among the emphatic though fleeting white horizontals of the sea to north-west of Fladday. It came wavering down the coast of Scarp and anchored in the comparatively calm water about twenty yards out from the mooring of our own boat. We waved, thinking perhaps he might be intending to come ashore. A middle-aged man in a rumpled khaki-coloured cotton suit waved back, but then busied himself about his boat, and went below – to have some food, probably, or some sleep, perhaps. In our solitude,

105

this waving to a stranger, and keeping an eye on him, was our only social contact with the outside world for two days. It is amazing how quickly you learn, on desert islands, the value of all people. There are no nonentities and no bores. One is pleased to see absolutely anyone, even in the distance.

As the tide ebbed the breakers across the sound became steeper, and their force was reaching and rocking the stranger's boat violently. Obviously he couldn't know how much worse the waves might become, so he came on deck and pulled up his anchor to shift into deeper water, just beyond this point. This too he must have found an uncomfortable berth, with the benefit of waves from both directions. So he set off down the sound. He may have intended to batter his way round Husinish point, and go the five or so miles up past Govig, to the lovely, sheltered harbour of Amhuinnsuidhe. If he already knew the place, what a heaven it must have appeared in his mind's eye. Flowery margins to satin water, moored lobster boats resting on undisturbed reflections. The crofter's cattle grazing at the sea's edge, and the young girls who are in charge of them following them up the hillsides at milking time. Even the ugly nineteenth century castle, full of anachronistic gentry, gives the scene a symbol of security; and maybe the yachtsman was at home in such castles. We had no way of knowing.

We could only see his mast wobbling through about forty degrees above the island's edge, beyond the schoolhouse, and then it disappeared behind the low, grey crouch of the mission. When the yacht reappeared it was riding the bucking bronco of the swell beyond the south-east corner of Scarp. As we watched through binoculars it looked really alarming. It would be dangerous to go on and dangerous to turn: but it did turn and came back to anchor again in our far-from-calm harbour. The yachtsman must have thought himself in a watery hell, with white-topped walls bearing down from the North, and the broken roarers rounding the corner to the South, with an agitated cakewalk of water between.

The news of Radio 4 was full of the Notting Hill Carnival. It was difficult to imagine a quarter-of-a-million people crammed into a space smaller than Scarp, which seems crowded with thirty or so people on shore. There was no need for gratuitous human violence here, where all men are brothers because absence makes the heart grow fonder. We could well understand the primitive law of hospitality to all strangers. Out yachtsman might have been Lord Lucan himself; we would have welcomed him had he come ashore, though he might have disdained our welcome, as we hadn't been formally introduced

106

and didn't wear any sort of tie at all, let alone the right sort of old school one. But he proved to be the Flying Dutchman, and, as the tide turned, and, over deeper water, the waves undulated without breaking, he wavered off northward again, the way he had come.

Norman and Jacob had both gone out in separate directions, to draw the rough sea from the lee of some sheltering rock, and Ben and I went down to the south end together, to watch the great walls of water riding in to smash over the rocks. In one deeply gashed inlet of the cliff, under the Suicide Mushrooms that grow large as dinner plates and untouched on a steep ledge, the spume was ascending with the trapped wind that could go no other way but upward, soaring like rebellious snow. It whirled about, to settle on the clifftop heather where its clustered bubbles glistened, trembled and, one by one, disappeared. Ben and I were gradually wet through by the salt rain, though the sun was now shining intermittently, and it was really not raining at all.

Walking back along the shore as the tide rose, there were rainbows coming and going in the blown spray of the waves which were pouncing on the beach at various angles, sending out swift catspaws of water. There were fragmentary rainbows in the sky, also. God's broken promises. And the Welshmen crossed the sound and rode past towards their pots by Fladday. I thought they were taking a risk, though they appeared to leap the breakers to northward with the ease of an Olympic hurdler. "They take risks for their livelihood," I thought, "and for more than a livelihood." I remembered island gossip of thousands of pounds changing hands for a few weeks' lobsters. I could not then know that later that evening they were unable to get back and took refuge in the sheltered water of Cravadale, where they anchored their boat and scrambled home, very late, by the cliff path.

★

The following day seemed convalescent. "If it goes on like this" we thought, "tomorrow will be ideal for our crossing." "Force four," had said the midnight forecast of the winds' race round the map of Scotland today. We spent a normal sort of morning, though the boys at last took up the mooring stones and brought the boat ashore onto its rusty trailer. During their long Summer on the seabed the stones had grown tall forests of weed, and one of our ropes was worn almost through. Knots originally tied by Angus MacInnes, now dead, would have to be replaced, though Norman had liked to regard them as a kind of memorial to the last of the islanders, who had passed on to

107

us a few of his island skills, without which we would have been helpless.

I spent the morning hastily painting our backdoor blue and the front windows white, to keep the winter weather out during our absence. The last coat of paint had cracked up into albino cornflakes, and much of the wood was bare. There was low cloud brushing the mountains opposite, and a threat of rain, so I hurried with this task. As I worked I saw over my shoulder the Welshmen rolls-roycing down the sound with a stack of kreels astern. And the yacht returned again; so it was still afloat. Its sails were rigged today, and it tacked against the southerly wind. This time it would reach the paradise harbour. It undulated over the waves as though riding on mere roundabout horses, and made its way south-westward, out of sight.

As I was getting lunch I heard the weather forecast. Winds moderating, southerly; freshening South East, or East, force five or six: but they will return to the South West by morning. Becoming strong, gale-force in places.

"So we must leave now" we all realised. "Tomorrow is going to be worse, not better." I rounded up Jacob, who was out perched on a seashore rock, like a cormorant, drawing, and we all ate a lavish meal in preparation for five or six hours of work ahead, though my own appetite had been partially destroyed by tension. I did not really relish the prospect of setting out on that sea in the rubber dinghy. We leave the larger boat tied down ashore on the island, having used it for transporting all the luggage over, and we ourselves cross over in the inflatable, which we then deflate and take home with us.

So now Norman and the boys launched the boat and stowed it with our belongings – mostly ready-packed – and they took them over to Husinish. I sorted out the house, folding the blankets round a random scattering of mothballs, for we had slept our last night on Scarp this year. I made sure there was no food left in the pantry. Rashly, just after lunch, I had packed the remaining tins of evaporated milk and the last of the bread, flour and rice in a cardboard box to go over the sound and be useful on the homeward journey. So we would have to leave that evening whatever happened. I was remembering what we had so often observed, that weather forecasts for our part of the Hebrides were usually a day late. We would be told what the weather was about to do when it had already just done it.

The chimney-cowls on the old Post Office are our windsocks. When their black mouths gape straight at us the wind is southerly. If they face to our left, as we look at them from the house, the wind is south-west; if to our right, it is south-east. The chimney-cowls' two mouths were saying "O, O," straight at us; then wavering to say "O, O," towards Cravadale and Lewis. The wind was more south-west than south, and no amount of wishful thinking could make it south-east or east. I began to be worried, and the adrenalin started to flow. I tried to work it off, and went down to help pull in the boat when it came back. We had to haul the boat, on its trailer, along the track of boulders along the edge of the beach. This had once been a grassed-over stony road fit to drive the old island Landrover along, but the Winter before last had washed it away. We had put back a ledge of boulders in a long afternoon of backbending, lifting and clunking the heavy rocks into place, and last Winter had treated our primitive road quite kindly. But it was a rough ride for the boat-trailer. We brought four rusty corrugated-zinc sheets, and laid them in front of the trailer-wheels. When we had pushed the trailer as far as we could on this, we brought the back sheets round to the front, and pushed on.

At last the boat was dragged up into the safest place we could find for it, and tied down. The boys cleaned the Johnson engine in a barrel of water. They and I carried the protesting and jagged zincs back up to the house, and stowed them away over the firewood store, weighted down with stones.

I glanced at the Post Office cowls again. South-southwest. I was still full of apprehension. The wind was not very strong, but neither was the sea very calm, and any south-west wind serves to encourage it in roughness.

When alone in the mothball-scented house I am reduced to prayer. I have changed into my sea-trousers and all the shirts and jerseys that I wish to take home, and I kneel down by the window – one may as well do it properly – and pray for a change of wind. "But who do you think you are?" I ask myself; "a middle-aged Joan of Arc? You can't go asking for changes of wind, or for any particular thing. That's not what prayer is for. Anyway, you don't believe in God." I don't use that word, but I do believe in a vast power which wakens into consciousness like a tree breaking into blossom. We are manifestations of the urge to consciousness of this power. We are eyes, blossoms, nerve-endings; and our desire to remain conscious has the great power behind it. We are also part of the power. Our intensity of being, our concentration (one might call it prayer) can affect the course of events. It is no inconsiderable part of the great forces of creation. We are not mere god-lice, or passengers in the universe, like ticks on an Eagle. We are more like individual dowles of the Eagle's plumage, or cells

Mountain by the sea – rocks – stormy weather – Hebridean Study

in its eye. We take part in the direction of events. We are at least among the infinite legs of the Spiral Millipede, and have a part to play in its climb through time and space. But this does not mean that our desperate will to survive can change the direction of the wind. You should not pray for any particular material event to take place, or help yourself to any free wishes. There is that W.W. Jacobs story called 'The Monkey's Paw'. An elderly couple wish, by the power of the mummified paw, for a certain large sum of money; and a few days later they are granted this exact sum of money as compensation for the death of their only son, who has been caught in a machine and killed at the factory. We may get our wishes, but gratification will bring snags. Nothing is free. Euphoria is not on, it always smacks of hubris. But I am feeling far from hubristic, being ludicrously on my knees, praying for a safe crossing of the sound while the sea undulates like a flapping sheet and the wind refuses to blow seriously from any direction but the south-west.

"What may I pray for?" I wonder, and I try to empty my mind of present emergencies. The possibilities resolve themselves into a phrase sufficiently ambiguous to be undeniable. I pray to be a continuing force. This is inevitable. Even if we were all to be finished together, and I were to die childless, and all my unpublished poems be lost, there would still be the eddies I have been unconsciously making, and the effects I have been unconscious of causing, by forgotten words and casual acts. Energy is never lost, only transferred from agent to agent. I have been on the earth, and gone up and down in it. I have had a fair crack of the whip. And this cannot be taken away from me. What's done cannot be undone.

The overdressed Joan of Arc clambered to her feet feeling calmer. Imminence of execution certainly concentrates the mind wonderfully. The continuing force made a last brew of hot tea for the others, who had finished settling the boat, and we drank up the last of the pseudo-milk in it. It was already seven o'clock.

We stepped into the dinghy accompanied by a wail or two from the cat, who quietened down almost at once when he discovered that his basket wrapped up in a parcel of plastic was keeping him dry and comfortable. On the journey to Scarp he howled all the way and arrived as wet as a substandard otter, all spiky with salt water and very cross. So this time we had wrapped the cat-basket round with a large sheet of polythene, and tied it with string. Having taken up all of our positions, with myself in front as ballast and breakwater, as usual, we committed the insanity of pushing off from the jetty. The engine started at the first pull, and we were afloat and on our way. All fear, now that the die was cast, left me.

As we rounded the point by the harbour we met the secondary swell, the diminished but continuing force of the waves that had already battered the cliffs across the sound. This was some indication of what would be in store when we left the shelter of the island. But, several hours earlier, when I had been waiting for Norman and the boys to come back from Husinish with the boat, after taking the luggage over, I had seen a line of dark marks, far out towards the bridge of breakers, labouring against wind and current. I couldn't see what it was. The binoculars were already over the sound. Was it an otter with young, in single file? A Loch Ness monster of some kind? A dolphin, porpoise, whale or shark? It resembled none of these, but the line of spikes wavered onward as though it was a swimming snake with a line of sharp fins down its back. It struggled and made little headway. Each time I looked out, curiously, it seemed to be in the same place. Then our boat came up the sound with our largest engine going full-throttle, and the spikes scattered. They were young ducks. Now, two or three hours later, they were still in the sound, a little ahead of us, but they scattered and dived as we caught them up and passed them. They were the darkish, low-in-the-water Scoters. "If these mere ducks could do it, then so can we," I thought, though I realised that ducks are proverbially well-suited to water; but we were bigger, and had all this technology at our command (to let us down), and humanity's famous survival-kit of versatility and adaptability; though we are not yet adapted to living underwater unfortunately.

We passed the southern point of the island, keeping well away from the broken water over the rocks, and we met the Atlantic swell obliquely. We travelled due south; it travelled due north-east. The first few waves were not at all bad, but we made very little progress, and seemed to stand in the same relation to the south-east corner of Scarp for a very long time while the Seagull forty-plus engine laboured valiantly. Each wave gave us such a mighty shove sideways and backwards as it came on, that much of our energy was used in making up for this displacement. Then came a really tall hill of water, as high as a terrace of houses. Imagine the spreading suburbs of a town actually moving at you, terrace by terrace, across the weedy fields of water. But we soared buoyantly up to the wave's steep roof, over its ridge, and slid down the other, shallower, side. "We couldn't do with too many like that one", I thought; but it was followed by a great wave like Hadrian's Wall, complete with the ridge of rock that it is built on, turned from defence to aggression, and travelling inexorably into

Scotland. This was followed by the Great Wall of China, made of water, the Berlin Wall, made of water, the Iron Curtain, the language barrier, and all the walls in creation, rushing at us by turns. Luckily, they did not come tumbling down on us, but collapsed under their own weight a few hundred yards further on in their progress, so we rode them triumphantly, though always in apprehension of the next. I found myself thinking, quite irrelevantly, and probably unscientifically, having no understanding of the problems, "What a marvellous place for generating electricity". We were picking our feeble way across a power of irresistibly continuing force. If only it could be harnessed it could light up the entire Hebrides; or the whole map of Scotland, perhaps.

Out in the boat I have observed, of the sea and myself, that there are calm and silky seas whereon you fear nothing at all; and there are choppy seas whereon you fear to get wet. Then there are seas whereon you are wet and cold, and fear drowning, but there are other seas, which throw bucket after bucket of cold salt water at you, and you are wet right through to the skin but quite unafraid, realising that the sea is only playing. But this was not a playful sea. It was a serious sea: far too serious to notice us at all in its obsessed surge towards smash-up under the cliffs.

Sometimes, when, from the shore, one watches little boats crossing the sound, they disappear altogether into the troughs of the waves and pretend to have sunk, until, to everyone's relief, they bob up again. From where we were, at sea in the dinghy, it was the dry land that seemed to have disappeared altogether while we were cradled in the wave-troughs, and hemmed about by obstructing walls of water. It was as though the sea had altogether overwhelmed the land, which no longer existed. But we climbed hill after hill of water, and were able to reassure ourselves that the shore was still there before we plunged again into the valley.

And the dry land was drawing nearer. At last the Husinish shore appeared quite definitely closer than Scarp, and rapidly it drew into clear focus. We made steady headway now that we were protected from the worst of the swell by Husinish point. Then the sun dropped below the ceiling of cloud that had hovered over us all day, to shine horizontally at the Harris mainland hills. The sky to the west was clear, and the hills were floodlit. After scrambling ashore onto the jetty from a boat that was going up and down like a yo-yo on the waves, and then going down to help drag it up the bit of sandy beach where Norman and Ben decided to land it, I walked over to the postman's house to pick up any last post, and to say our farewells.

The knapweed growing in the uncut meadow-grass by the path was a vivid crimson-purple in the evening light, and the hills were luminous green and pink with heather. How beautiful everything is, I thought, especially the dry land now so reassuringly under my feet.

Rainbow Plantation

Now is the rainbow season –
Rainbow seed
Planted in time's beginning
Grows at light's speed.

Seemingly without season
The fluted bridges sprout
From Brenish and from Taransay
So ancient mountains greet.

The slow clouds, stapled down
By rainbow's piercing, meet
After circuitous travelling
Since Creation's date.

Even that distant bird –
A mote in rainbow light –
Has not arrived by chance
But arduous spiral flight

Out of the shadowed seas
Where rainbows germinate
To bloom, over these Hebrides,
In ecstasies of white.

Scottish Inshore Waters Weather Report

A shadowy map of sea-torn and scattered islands,
fixed in the undulation and slide of ocean,
frays dark holes in the gleaming and seamless sea, where
          mackerel's shoaling.

Machrihanish – three miles – and pressure steady:
trawlers wake the water with luminous scars,
tearing the self-repairing skin of the groundswell
          rising and falling.

Tiree – shoals of stars in the treacle-black water;
drizzling curtains draw and erase sea-mountains:
oceanic ablutions lave birdroost islands.
          Breakers come rolling.

Stornoway – sea-town people go pray for your ships, the
night-fishing fleet is at sea and the south-west rising:
storm force gusts in the Hebrides, also the Minches:
          one thousand, falling.

Cape Wrath – here the remains of some young woman's lover
drift in the current, nameless: rain sweeps the water:
storm-wrack, uprooted sea-tangle, torn nets and a rudder –
          rising and falling.

Lerwick: one-thousand-and-ten, and rising. Seal Skerry:
waistless mothers, reclining on tidewashed stones,
suckle fat pups, with shrill, electronic crooning,
          sirenlike calling.

Aberdeen Dyce, and Lucas; far from this island
where, in the treacherous rush and backsliding of waters,
watching by lamplight, alone, I hear lost sea-voices
          long for winds' lulling.

The Island Tax

for David Fry

His Majesty the Sea demands –
    every decade or so – an Island Tax,
and snatches children from the sands
    or fishermen from rocks;
        just when we least expect it
        he takes a boat and wrecks it.

Between implacable demands
    his hushing lulls us almost into sleep.
The Sea Lord feeds us, condescends
    to lend the roof across his deep
        as playground and provider;
        his minions fill our larder.

He salivates around our shores
    and undermines the cliff from which I hear
his waves in sea-caves, slamming doors
    on grumbling Minotaur:
        someone must pay protection
        to our great neighbour's faction.

The papery tufts of Sea-pink shake;
    the sea-skin shudders and a sail lies down;
in waters quiet as a lake
    unwary swimmers drown;
        out in those wide blue spaces
        assassins leave no traces.

The King conscripts his forces
    commanded by a gale-force Southwest wind;
long ranks of white-plumed horses
    advance against the land:
        but that's an ancient story,
        my tale's contemporary.

The Mafioso Sea has sent
    his tall green debt-collector to our door
to execute an innocent

whom we shall see no more.
    Swifter than cobras, breakers
    rush over rocks to take us.

Fly-by-Nights

At first we were a little hurt to find ourselves known by this title. I don't know whether it is more or less derogatory than that of 'white settlers', which is how the English or Lowlander New Hebrideans are known to the indigenous Long Islanders. But 'Fly-by-night' does imply cowardice, fine-weather friendship, and compromise: and it implies that we ought to stay, or else we ought not to have come. But are the old, absentee Hebrideans not also Fly-by-night, and of a darker dye? Is not Scarp empty because its people fled from the twilight of crofting and the night of unemployment to the ceaseless shiftwork of the towns? They fled from the night of oil-lamps to the day of electricity, and from the night of the past and its old ways into the featureless glare of the future.

But 'Fly-by-night' can also be taken to mean 'Summer visitors', like the wheatears, the cuckoo or the swallows. We are a kind of swallow-substitute, since the actual swallows have not discovered the Long Island. It would be a good thing if they did, since they eat insects on the wing and they might reduce the midge population a little – if the infinite can be reduced. As substitute swallows we eat no insects, unfortunately; but we do employ ourselves almost as seriously as the swallows, and get a great deal of work done in our second-hand house.

When we bought it we designated one room as bedroom, and one as general living-room; one is, inescapably, the kitchen, and the fourth is the studio. Spare bedrooms were supplied by tents until a year or two ago when we built on another room, without asking anyone for planning permission. A bonanza of good timber had drifted onto the beach, and MacDonald's shed had blown down, so the wood was supplied free, though we had to buy the necessary corrugated zinc. For window-glass we used the windscreen of the derelict and much cannibalised Landrover that used to help to pull the last islanders' boat ashore. But I did not set out to describe our sleeping arrangements, nor our building materials, but to make clear that we come to Scarp to work.

When Norman repaired the rusting zinc sheets of the north end of the house, he replaced some of them with corrugated perspex, and removed a panel of wood on the inside, thus making a good north light. When the studio thus created was complete he made a work-bench for himself and a writing-table for me, both out of planks bought from the crofters' stores in Tarbert. I resurrected a square, flat-seated crofter chair from a fallen house, and with paper and ballpoint pen I was in business. And Norman had brought with him brushes and pigments, oils and canvas, and the other ingredients of painting, and he was in business too, only rather more so. On the desk, set in a working-corner of the bedroom, I have written thousands of words, including numerous poems, and in the studio, as well as outside among the crags and down by the shore, Norman has painted innumerable watercolours as well as several large oils. While the last two Scarp families were still living on either side of us, he stayed through the Summer from May to September, like a proper swallow, and painted exploratory designs for a mural commission which has since been completed in St. Anselm's Church, Kennington, London. So a painting adorning the length of the nave of a church in London has its roots in Scarp. And certain paintings related to it are out and about in the world. A series of studio watercolours called the 'Oval Marine Passion', painted within sight of Scarp's serpentine sound was exhibited in the Serpentine Gallery, Hyde Park, and many watercolours of sea and mountains have hung on the walls of the Royal Academy (of all places), and other London Galleries. The name of Scarp must figure in the catalogues of many art-collections:- 'Seabirds diving, Scarp', 'The Atlantic, from Scarp' 'A Vision of Islands, the St. Kildas, from Scarp'. These are typical titles.

And somewhere are my own watercolours that have wandered off into the world: 'Scarp Weeds', 'Harebell machair, Scarp', 'Scarp Weedscape'. These are my sort of titles. I find the bright, fragile forms of flowers, so close beside that dark and indifferent sea, particularly moving. Their colours seem to have more than the usual luminosity of flowers. Beside that threat their mortality and pathos are underlined. And through the medium of print some of my Scarp poems have been to both ends of the earth at once. So Scarp has been in the export business lately. It has been exporting its own image.

It has also been dabbling in the tourist industry; for the twenty-year-old, roughcast bungalow nearby, bought by a man who works for the gas board in the Midlands, is often let, for fortnights at a time, to exotics from the south – even the deep south: Surrey, Kent or Somerset. The chief crime reporter from a leading daily paper, an army officer with his family, a retired naval officer, a manure tycoon, a personnel manager from a Midlands factory, an industrial chemist, several teachers, nurses, dentists, a professor of art-history from a white-tile university, an economist who thought it immoral to live in villages, and a happy band of medical students – these have all lived action-packed fortnights in Annie and Murdo McInnes' discarded bungalow.

Down in the Mission House the population is more stable. There the minister and his wife, who used to come in the old days of the community, still come for a few weeks of sabbath quiet during most Summers. Some friends of theirs, a doctor and his wife, also come to stay for quite long periods, and the wife goes woolgathering, dyes her gatherings with crottle scraped from the rocks, and spins, knits and even weaves on an improvised loom made from an old fishbox. The same woman has also cured the skins of mink caught by their dog, and her husband has made a splendid wooden armchair from driftwood.

Nearly all these summer migrants have brought children who will carry away with them, as part of their mental furniture for the rest of their lives, the image of Scarp and the idea of a possible way of life.

But at each Summer's end, as we say 'goodbye' to the island – (and we are often the last to go) – we know it may be a final parting. For we may 'Fly-by-night' indeed. Who can tell what the year to come holds in store? And we may cease to come for the same reason as that which caused the old Scarpese to leave the island: because we ourselves are getting older and our children will leave us. I am, in fact, amazed that they should have come away with us for so long. Certainly, without the boys, we would be unable to get our boat into the water, or out of it. Already, this year, one of the boys went off to a holiday job half-way through our stay, and just the three of us had to haul the boat, on its rusty trailer, along the rocky shore to its winter resting place; and it was as much as we could do. Besides – the rest of the world is calling.

So, as the days shorten, and the equinoctial gales sweep over us, roaring and hissing in the ashtrees outside this our Yorkshire house, I think of the similar sound of great seas breaking over Scarp, eroding just a little more of the crumbling shore every year. The waves explode in hollow places of the cliff and sound as though the last inhabitant has left the island's door open and swinging in the wind. It keeps banging and banging, and there is no one to close it. Of course the sheep are still there, nibbling the turf down to the bone, and the gannets and cormorants are there; but there is no one to name them. Rocks, caves and waterfalls escape from man's language-net, and the island becomes a menacing dream of abstract mineral forms. Mountains, capes and bays revert to anonymity. Their histories escape

121

them. No one can tell what may have happened here. There are no witnesses.

The wind screams high over Strone Romul, removing the shallow mountain-top tarns from their stony beds, in a battle between the horizontal force of air and the vertical force of gravity. Gravity wins when the wind tires, but there are large eroded patches on the eastern shores of these tarns. And Juniper Horizontalis moulds itself to the contours of the ground; having learnt too well that he that is down need fear no fall, it forgets that it is a tree.

In the sheltered lap of the island, houses fall into ruins. No smoke flies out at right angles from the chimneys, drawing up peat-fires inside. No songs or tales are heard round the hearths. No child bends over his homework, ensuring the future.

And thinking about the childless island, I realise afresh what poets mean by an objective correlative. Does the island's image haunt me because my children, too, are grown and flown, and my lap and arms are empty?

But I do not intend to spend twenty years looking backward. I look forward to a new career. I intend to live a new kind of life as my unimpeded self, god willing, and am wound up and ready to go. There are other things for women to do besides rear children, and I hope to do them, for I am an optimist.

And because I am an optimist I cannot believe that Scarp will not have an inhabited and useful future. Perhaps it was necessary that the ground should be cleared, so that life might begin again in a more modern way. I refuse to refrain from the hope that Scarp Desolate may, in due course, prove to be Scarp Fallow.

Map

This map is only paper,
its sea is ink
that parches the eye's craving
for distances to drink.

We rustle paper salad
peppered well with print
thirsting for the mystery
the symbols hunt.

Words beckon to the rose,
contours lasso the hill,
seeking to lure the real
into the skull:

then, because the presence
we apprehend is flame
we quench it with the spell
of naming, to a name.

About the Author

ANNA ADAMS was educated at Harrow Art School, and Hornsey College of Art, and has worked as a designer, a freelance artist and an art teacher. These days she devotes the greater part of her creative energies to writing, and has had three collections of poetry published by Peterloo: *A Reply to Intercepted Mail* in 1979, *Trees in Sheep Country* in 1986 and *Nobodies* in 1990. Littlewood brought out another one, *Dear Vincent*, in 1986, and this contains poems that are mainly about art. *Island Chapters* contains most of the poems and prose that she wrote on or about Scarp, in the Outer Hebrides where – for more than ten years – she and her husband spent much time.

She is at present poetry editor of *The Green Book*, and divides her time between North Yorkshire and London.

About the Artist

NORMAN ADAMS studied painting at Harrow School of Art and the Royal College of Art. Since the early Fifties he has had regular one-man shows in London, and exhibited widely all over England and Scotland. He has had large retrospectives at the Gulbenkian Gallery, Kensington, at the Whitechapel Art Gallery, at the Third Eye in Glasgow and at the Royal Academy of Arts in 1988. Commissions include decor and costumes for ballets at Covent Garden and Sadler's Wells, murals for St. Anselm's Church, Kennington, and a series of Stations of the Cross in the R.C. Church of Our Lady of Lourdes, in Milton Keynes.

He works both from nature and the imagination, often painting subjects of a religious/philosophical nature.

He was elected ARA in 1967, RA in 1972, and Keeper of the Royal Academy in 1986 and 1989.